Beautiful Courage

A Young Woman's Journey West

The journal and letters of
Kathleen Margaret McClellan
April 26-September 22, 1852

Diane M. Covington-Carter

Beautiful Courage
A Young Woman's Journey West

Published by Marshall and McClintic Publishing,
Nevada City, CA 95959

Diane Covington-Carter's back cover photo
by Carrie Dobbs, Takaka, New Zealand

Cover artwork and book illustrations by Susan R. Whiting
Layout by Margie Baxley
Cover Layout by Margaret Campbell

This book is set in Times New Roman Type Text
Printed in the United States of America
First Edition June 15, 2019

ISBN-13: 978-0-9910446-6-5
ISBN-10: 0-9910446-6-5

To all the pioneer women who showed such
Beautiful Courage
as they journeyed West

Author's note

Between the years 1841 and 1869, over 250,000 pioneers headed west on the California Trail. Some were searching for gold and riches, others wanted opportunity, freedom and adventure. Many came for the rich farmland and milder climate. The California Trail's popularity peaked in 1852.

The journey to California was roughly 2,000 miles and would take a typical emigrant family five months to complete the trip.

Most pioneers began their journey at "jumping off towns" along the Missouri River. When they crossed to the west bank of the Missouri River, they were leaving the United States and entering unorganized territory.

There were no roads, towns, houses, stores or any means of communication for the next five months.

As the emigrants traveled west, the wagon was their only home and shelter. They mostly walked the 2,000 miles in order to spare the draft animals pulling their wagons, which contained all their food and supplies.

They faced many perils on their journey. Dangerous river crossings and diseases such as cholera, which could break out and take lives within a day. Also, starvation, accidents with guns and sometimes hostile Indians, crossing deserts and keeping their animals alive and well. It is estimated that one in ten emigrants died and were buried along the trail.

The pioneers who traveled west hoping for better lives and broader opportunities, not only showed great courage, but they changed the course of American history. They expanded the boundary of America from the Atlantic to the Pacific Ocean and their settling of the American West gave the United States access to vast new sources of agricultural and mineral wealth.

This story chronicles one family's journey west in 1852, told through the eyes of Katie, age 13.

I hope that you enjoy the story.

Diane Covington-Carter,
June 15, 2019

Monday, April 26, 1852

Quincy, Illinois

I look out from our canvas covered wagon and feel the heartache of good-bye. Early this morning, I watched our farm fade into the rose light of dawn and my grandma and grandpa, my aunt and uncle and cousins become smaller and smaller in the distance.

Grandma waved a white hanky–she said I'd be able to see it longer and she was right. That white cotton square moved back and forth through the trees long after the people faded and blurred.

Just when we pulled away, my cousin Carrie, her face streaked with tears, ran behind the wagon and held out a bouquet of sweet peas, tied to a pouch of letters. I reached out for them and as our hands touched, I wanted to just hang on and bring her with me. But I couldn't. It was the last time we'll touch for a very long time. I don't want to think that it might be forever.

Mama gave me this new writing book today when she noticed my tears. It could be a place to air my soul, she said. She also said I might feel excited again about going West to California, but just to let the feelings be, till they use themselves up. I begin this new journal as I begin a new life, rolling toward the West, away from everything I have ever known.

I went and sat by Mama in the front of the wagon. She was holding Peter, my brother, who is ten. As she reached over to hold me too, the bouncing of the wagon wheels made it hard to hug and we ended up laughing as we bumped into each other. Her soft, warm body reassured me. We are leaving behind everything we know, for a dream called California, Mama, Papa, Peter and me.

My Uncle Peter–that's Papa's younger brother–and his wife Aunt Sarah decided to come with us on the journey. They have two little boys, two and four, Matthew and Jason, and their wagon is ahead of ours on the road.

We also brought along my horse, Burt, our milk cow Rose, and our dog Nellie. Actually, Papa thought Nellie was too old to come with us and so we tried to leave her behind, but she followed us for an hour and wouldn't go home. Guess she wants to be a pioneer too. I'm so glad. I didn't want to leave Nellie— she was born about the same time as I was, so she is 13½ too. So Papa gave in and said Nellie could come along.

Four strong oxen pull our wagon. Papa raised and groomed them for the trip. The lead ox is Tom. He's the oldest and strongest and I think he is so special. I want to pat him and talk to him every day. Our survival is in his hands—he's pulling us all the way to California. Papa says we'll be walking most of the way to spare the oxen, except when it is raining too hard, like today.

Mama says to write about the things that I feel, so I am. She said that this can be the journal of my life, my own private story. And that it will be special to have been a pioneer, so writing about it as we go will help us to remember later and to be able to tell the stories.

Right now, I can only think about the life that I left behind. What will I miss? First off, I will miss Carrie. We've known each other since we were babies, over thirteen years. I don't remember back that far, but that is what Mama says. My first memory, when I was about two and a half, has Carrie in it. We were eating strawberries in the garden on a hot summer day. They tasted so sweet and warm and the juice felt sticky on my face and hands.

Mama says we were a sight to see, all covered in berry juice and dirt, so she put us into the laundry tub by the well pump to wash us off. I remember splashing and laughing with Carrie in the tub, and the feel of the warm sun and the cool water on my skin.

In addition to being my cousin, Carrie has always and will always be, my bestest friend. I'm not sure bestest is a word, but this is my book, and bestest is better than best and so is Carrie to me.

We're traveling to the Mississippi River on our way to Independence Missouri, where we'll join twenty other wagons bound for California. They say tens of thousands are heading west like we are. Papa said he read that fifty thousand pioneers are going this year. I can't imagine that. What a journey this will be.

Mama says the past, present and future are all a part of each day. There's where you are, where you've been and where you're headed. She says where you are and where you're headed are the most important, but where you've been colors how you see the other two. Right now, I want to note down some of the "where I've been" as we begin our journey to California. But I don't want to miss out on today.

I'm going to write to Carrie every day I can and write in here, even briefly, too.

Love, Me

Monday, April 26, 1852
Leaving Day
Dear Carrie,

Oh how I miss you already. I'm afraid, excited and sad all at the same time. I can't remember being afraid and sad much before. Excited, yes, especially with you. Remember how we'd share our birthday celebrations--since we're only eight days apart? Ginger cakes with fresh cream, dancing and jumping off the haystacks in the barn—oh such fun.

And riding together on old Bessie through the meadow and then swimming in the pond? She'd even let us lead her into the pond and then stand on her back and jump in. What a sweet horse. Give her a carrot and a pat for me and remind her that she can be proud that her son, Burt, is going to California with us.

It was harder than I thought it would be to say goodbye. As much as I think I want to go, I can't imagine what my life will be like now, without you in it. It feels like all my memories, I shared with you, even like our hearts overlap some. I've laughed more with you than with anyone else in the world. And I think you've seen me cry more than anyone, except maybe Mama. As I write to you, I can pretend that I'm talking with you and right now, that calms me.

Today we're riding in the wagon. Because of the rain, the mud is up to our ankles. The poor oxen, it's so slow and hard for them.

But it's pleasant jostling along and it gives me time to write. Except that my handwriting jumps up and down with each bump. Will you ever be able to read this? I hope so. Then you can imagine the wagon ride and all that is happening to me here, so far from you.

I look about our rolling home. The hickory bows bend over the top and blend down into the sides of our wagon bed, the wagon I helped Papa to build last winter in the barn. The canvas cover Mama and I made keeps the light spring rain off of us right now. We rubbed it with Linseed oil and beeswax to protect us from the elements, but I'm shivering. At least the rain isn't coming in.

As I look out the back of the wagon, it's like I'm looking out a round window onto the world passing by. I can see an apple orchard, with the pink blossoms opening to white and smell their sweet fragrance. If it was quiet, I might be able to hear the bees buzzing in and out of the blossoms, but the creaking of the wagon drowns out all other sounds.

Mama says to save up letters till we find someone going back. So I will. Your sweet peas fill the wagon with the smell of home and my heart with love for you. I'm saving the letters you gave to me as a special treat–I haven't read one yet. As I listen to the rain pattering on the wagon, I send you thoughts of love.
Your cousin, Katie
P.S. It should be fun to float on a river. Then the animals can rest, too.

Carrie's letters and the sweet peas

Tuesday, April 27, 1852
We're like a gypsy train, our two wagons, our animals and us. Some folks shake their heads at us, like we're crazy. Others want to ask us all kinds of questions. Papa tries to be polite, but we have to keep moving.

On this journey, the animals reign because they pull us along every mile. We'll choose our stopping places for them, where they have good grass and water. Last night, our first night out, we all crammed into the wagon to sleep. It was too wet and

10

muddy to sleep out. Tonight, we're camped near a farmhouse and the owners, a doctor and his wife, have been very gracious to us. They've invited us to sleep in their house and to eat at their table. Once we get out on the prairie, there won't be any houses to sleep in, just our wagon, tent and the open sky for our roof.

I have a few moments to write just as the sun sets over a grove of old oak trees. They remind me of my favorite old oak tree at home. I called her Mrs. Oak and loved to lean against her. I've been writing a journal for almost two years now. My favorite place to write used to be next to Mrs. Oak down by the stream.

In the winter, she lost all her leaves and on clear days, the sunlight streamed down on me, warming me. In summer, she shaded me. Fall, her leaves provided padding as I sat under her with the sun peeking through the spaces where the leaves used to be. Papa made us a swing from a board and rope and two of us could fit on that together. What fun we had on that swing.

When the snow came, it piled up on the swing and made the swing look lonely. One winter day, Carrie and I cleaned the snow off the swing and jumped on, gliding back and forth as the soft snowflakes tickled our faces. I could imagine Mrs. Oak smiling at us as we laughed and squealed and pumped high into the air.

I liked to put my arms around Mrs. Oak, with my heart right up against her and feel how she is alive, just like I am. I couldn't reach around her, not even part of the way. Sometimes I couldn't tell if it was my heart or hers, which I felt. When I hugged her, I felt her strength run into me, like she wanted to help me. She did, too. I always would take a pencil and my tablet with me and write down the wise and simple things she told me.

11

The last time I sat under her before we left, she told me to be quiet and listen. I wasn't sure what she meant. So I sat quiet and listened. Then I heard the wild geese calling to each other as they returned after the long winter. When I looked up, I saw their perfect V formation in the sky.

Then I heard a squirrel scampering up the tree and calling out to its mate; it seemed excited by spring. I saw what Mrs. Oak meant–to pay attention to life all around me and within me. To discover. And that I can do that best when I'm quiet and listen. That made good sense to me.

This journal can help me to pay attention to what is within and without on this great journey we begin to California. Right now, if I'm quiet and listen, I hear the creek near me gurgling and splashing, a bird singing high up in the branches and Mama calling me in to supper. Until tomorrow.

Love, Me

Wednesday, April 28, 1852

The doctor and his wife were real nice and didn't disapprove of going west. She gave us some cake and dried fruit to take along, but she made me miss grandma, already.

We're on a steamboat on the Mississippi River on our way to St. Louis. We loaded our wagons, our animals, and then ourselves and all our dreams. It's a good thing that dreams are light. What a crowded boat with everyone else headed west too. When we reach St Louis, then we'll be on the Missouri River to Independence, Missouri, where we'll meet up with the rest of our train, 22 wagons in all.

It's fun and soothing, floating on the broad river. It feels like I can breathe the freedom of our journey already in this air. The cool spring air rising off the river feels fresh. The rain has stopped for now.

After all the bustle to prepare to leave, I feel relaxed. Papa says to rest up now for the big journey. I like having lots of time to write. Time to complete my story, about my past, before we're moving over the prairie. We don't have as many chores right now as we did at home and as we will on the trail west. I milk Rose in the morning and evening and help Papa with the other animals. I like to help. The animals are a piece of home we brought with us and I'm glad to have them.

Since I have this time to write, I want to write about everyone in my family. Guess I'll start with myself.

I'm named after my Grandmama Kathleen, my Mama's Mama. We call her Grandmama because she's very formal. Whenever we went to see her, we had to be on our best manners. I didn't like that. She didn't even approve of giggling, thought it was silly. Well it is, and that is why I like it. It feels good to be silly. Grandmama looks like she could have used some more giggling in her life. I told Mama that and she said to be sure not to say that to Grandmama, but Mama knows what I mean.

Mama laughs a lot, especially with Papa, Peter and me. Mama isn't like Grandmama much. I guess it is special to have my grandmother's name. I wish I liked her more. Mama says I might like her when I'm older and understand life more. Mama is usually right about things. I'll have to wait and see.

But back to me. Even though I'm 13, I'm not very big. That is, I'm rather tall but not very round. Papa says I'm going to be tall, like Mama's side of the family. Mama is as tall as Papa. My Grandpapa (my Mama's Papa) is so tall that he has to bend over to come in and go out of most buildings. I like him. He's very sweet and kind of shy. When I was little, he used to pick me up and swing me around and I felt like I was on top of the world. Now I'm too big for that, but when he hugs me, I come up almost to his heart.

We lived on a farm, on the edge of the forest. Papa cleared the land himself, with the help of his two brothers, my Uncle Peter and Uncle Joshua. Uncle Peter and Aunt Sarah lived on one side of us with their two little boys and I helped Aunt Sarah out sometimes. She and Uncle Peter and the boys travel with us to California.

Uncle Joshua and Aunt Eliza lived on the other side of us. That's Carrie's Papa and Mama. Carrie has three little brothers, Paul, who is ten, John who is seven and Luke who is four. Peter liked to play with all of the cousins, especially Paul.

Papa's parents, Grandma Josie and Grandpa Graham, lived across the field. I so loved to visit my Grandma Josie. I called her Grandma "cross the fields" and could run over and see her anytime I wanted. I always helped her in the garden—she had so many different kinds of flowers and the best vegetable garden.

And then her chickens. She so loved her chickens and had over thirty hens and five roosters. It was so special to help her to gather the eggs when they were still warm and had a soft feather stuck to them. I so remember feeling the miracle of the warm, just laid egg in my cold hand on a chilly winter morning.

And each spring, the new little chicks would hatch and peck their way out of their shells. I'd check each day to see how many new ones had arrived. When they got a little bigger, we could hold them carefully—I'd hold them against my heart and stroke them gently and Carrie and I would love to hear their little cheeping sounds.

Our family all helped each other, living so close by, and we got together for all the holidays and had great celebrations. I can't imagine the holidays without them.

We had lots of wildlife that lived in the forest near us. The eagles were my favorites. I loved to watch them soar and swoop. They were so powerful and regal. They seemed wise to me, quiet, still and present. I always considered it good luck to see one.

There were also foxes, coyotes, bears, and families of deer, rabbits and squirrels. The deer were so graceful as they bounded along. The babies were especially cute, so shy, sticking right to their mothers.

On this trip, I've seen lots of deer families, especially at dusk near the river. I've also seen rabbits and squirrels. They feel like a little piece of home comforting me. I guess we'll see lots of wildlife out here on this journey. I'm glad of that. I'm watching for eagles.

Till tomorrow. Love, Me

Thursday, April 29, 1852
Dear Carrie,

We arrived at St. Louis. It's a big city, with boarded sidewalks and thousands of people running everywhere trading for the goods they needed, oxen to pull, the last pounds of flour. We went into a store called a mercantile, the largest store I have ever seen. So many colors of calico fabrics—oh what pretty dresses we could make.

There were all kinds of boots, the leather smelled so good, saddles and rifles and provisions for the trail—everything a person could ever need. I could have spent a whole day in that store just looking at it all. And the candy–I never knew there were so many flavors and kinds of candy in the world. Mama let us pick out one piece. I got a butterscotch and Peter chose a licorice stick. We bought a peppermint stick each for Matthew and Jason.

Then it was time to get back onto the boat and check on our animals. They seem fine with all this change. Maybe it is comforting for them to be together, like it is for us. Uncle Peter

15

and Aunt Sarah and the boys seem fine too. The little ones are not used to spending so much time all together—we usually have so many chores at home. They seem to think this is a special lark. I hope that it is. They loved their candy.

Now we're on the Missouri River heading toward Independence, Missouri, where we'll start our overland journey.

On this river, we're going against the current, so the crew have to work hard to keep us moving. Sometimes we get stuck on sand bars or have to maneuver around trees that got carried down with last winter's storms. Peter and I watch, fascinated. It's an adventure that is spoiled only by you not being here to share the fun.

This morning, the sun rose in a giant burst of pink and lavender, reflecting on the water. After the slow and difficult mud of our first few days in the wagon, it is so lovely to be on the water, even if we're going slowly sometimes. Papa and Mama have time to sit and rest, too, and that is so special. Nellie seems to like all the new smells.

We've all been reading. The captain of the steamboat has a wonderful store of books and has been sharing them with us. I'm devouring them and so writing less to you. Please forgive me, dear cousin, but the books are delicious.

He even has the newest books: Jane Eyre by Charlotte Bronte, Vanity Fair by Thackeray. Ralph Waldo Emerson's Nature and Essays and some of James Fennimore Cooper's which I'd read at Grandmama's: Leatherstocking Tales and The Spy. Peter is reading the Last of the Mohicans.

Will write more soon. Got to get back to Jane Eyre. Oh you must read it.

Love, Katie

16

Thursday, April 29. 1852

We're still on the river and I'm feeling peaceful. This brief time before the trail gives us time to rest, read and write. Today I want to write about Peter, my little brother who is ten. In France they say "he has 10 years." I find that interesting. I am learning French from Mama. She says it's important to know another language because it helps you to really know English. And that you can talk to people you could never talk to otherwise. Mama has even been to France once, but that was before she met Papa and of course before having us.

Us is Peter and me or is it Peter and I, I can never remember that rule. Peter's real cute and likes to tag along with me. Mostly I don't mind. He's funny in a boy sort of way. Mama says that boys and girls aren't that different, as far as their brains go and that girls can learn as well as boys. But still I learn a lot from comparing how Peter and I see the world.

I feel the world, in addition to seeing it. I sit back sometimes to feel what is going to happen, or at least to find out if I can feel it. Peter seems to see it and hear it and go at it with a fervor, kind of like a pig trying to get out of a gate. If I talk about this, Peter just looks at me and says, "Huh?" and shrugs his shoulders.

We used to go down to the stream after our chores. I loved to sense all the life that was a part of the stream. Peter would run ahead and would be throwing stones into the water before you could say "Jack Rabbit." I like to look at the stones and pick out a favorite. By that time, he's thrown in ten already.

But he's got lots of spunk, just like a little colt. We both like to run and play. We're fast friends.

Out on the farm, Peter and I were together a lot doing chores and our schoolwork, then playing. And of course, Carrie was there too and her brothers. There might be some new friends for us on the wagon train. That would be fun. Back to the luxury of books and reading before sleep.

Love, Me

Saturday, May 1, 1852

Another day on the Missouri River working our way toward Independence. It's slow going sometimes with the sand bars. Maybe all the weight of the wagons, livestock and us makes it hard for this boat. The men sure struggle to get us unstuck.

It smells like spring, a rich loamy smell of the earth and the river. I can see all the trees budding along the shore and some folks planting their fields. It is strange to think we won't be planting any crops this spring. We'll be walking west instead. I'll miss watching everything grow and the fun and the plenty of the harvest.

I was busy reading and missed a day of writing. But I notice that when I don't write, I still think about writing. It feels like I'm writing in my head, but it's not getting down on paper.

Today I want to write about Mama. Mama went to a special school for girls and traveled to Europe. She also taught school and loved that. Mama learned so many wonderful things in her education and now she shares them all with Peter and me.

Grandmama had big plans for Mama and wasn't pleased about Papa because she thought he wasn't good enough for Mama. But Mama and Papa really love each other and I can feel that and so should Grandmama. I would tell her that, but she'd just purse her lips and be cranky. So, when I went to see Grandmama, I mostly tried to be quiet.

That's not easy for me because I love to talk. Mama suggested I try writing because there's only so much talking a person can do and you have to have a listener. Writing, I can do all by myself and talk and listen all at once. Sometimes I write to find out what I really think about something, to sort it out.

Mama has dark brown hair, blue green eyes and dark long lashes. Peter and I have her lashes, though my eyes are green and Peter's are light blue like Papa's. She has the prettiest smile and her eyes light up when she gets excited. She's slim and tall and I'm proud she's my Mama.

Mama and I talk about what it was like when she was growing up. Everything is fancy at Grandmama's and Mama says it was always like that. They didn't get to run and play like we do, at least not while Grandmama was around. That doesn't make sense to me. I love the freedom of running through the meadow at full speed and not caring if I trip and do a somersault and get dirt on my clothes.

Mama had maids and other people helping out and sometimes they let her play and run when Grandmama was gone. But dinnertime, teatime, Sundays and most all the time, Mama had to be scrubbed clean, quiet, mind her manners and not mess things up, on and on. Doesn't seem like much fun to me. But in spite of it all, Mama loves to run and play and is loads of fun. She says sometimes she feels she is making up for lost times.

My middle name is Margaret. That's my mother's name. I'm glad that I have her name inside my name because, after all, I came from Mama. I have Papa's last name, so I have a little of both of them in my name.

But mostly, I love the way I can talk to Mama. Back at home, every night before I'd go to sleep, Mama and I would spend a little time, just the two of us. We'd sit real close, she'd brush my hair and we'd get to talk. I could count on that time with Mama and it was one of my favorite times of the day.

19

Mama would always remind me to say what I was most thankful for of the day. I'd always have a lot of special things to choose from: The fresh cream on the raspberries we picked for breakfast, sitting under the oak tree and reading and writing, singing with Mama as we washed the dishes, chasing Peter around the barn in a new game we made up, jumping from the loft into the haystack with Carrie, going with Papa through the fields and watching everything grow, the moon rising through my window as we'd sit and talk.

But of all the favorite things, I'd always be most thankful for my family, for the closeness we have. Mama says that's something to notice, isn't it? She's right. It isn't the things. Without the people and the love, things are empty and dull. Then I'd fall asleep saying everything else I remembered from the day that I loved.

Now it's harder to have that special time alone with Mama. But on this journey, as we move further west every day, further from everything familiar, I especially am thankful for my family. Tomorrow, I want to write about Papa.

Love, Me

Sunday, May 2, 1852

They say that tomorrow we'll reach Independence. Folks are getting nervous and excited. Once we leave this boat, the trail begins. Maybe having all this time to think has made some people scared. I asked Mama and Papa about that. They asked me if I was scared. I said I didn't think so because we were together. They're not scared, so I guess I'm not either.

If I do get scared, I can write about it. Writing seems to calm me down. I got my first journal on my twelfth birthday. But I really began writing a lot, when Mama said I could do English lessons by keeping my journal. She also said it could be private, that I didn't have to show it to her. But Mama would always understand and I don't have to hide anything from her.

So I've filled up several of these books already. They're packed away in trunks at Carrie's house. Someday we'll come back for them and so many other beloved things we left behind. Papa says we must think of our oxen and not weigh them down with too many belongings. We have our most important "belongings" right here, our family.

I had to leave behind my special dolls, with the clothes we made from scraps of my own dresses. I had a family of dolls and Papa made me a small cradle for the littlest baby. Back when I was seven, Grandma and I sewed a quilt for the baby in the cradle.

I miss my books. Some I'd read over and over and it was like visiting an old friend to snuggle up by the fire and begin again. And of course, I had to leave behind my rock collection. Rocks are heavy. I can't even collect any along the way. But I can admire them. My favorites are the ones that are split open, so you can see the colors of the layers, a magical interior landscape of silvers and blues.

We left everything but a few dishes, food, and Mama's best trunk from her childhood. That's where we packed all our clothes and special things. We've seen other wagons with rockers and all kinds of furniture strapped along. Papa says they'll probably leave those by the wayside. He's read accounts of people even leaving their wagons and walking the last stretch because their oxen died. Horrors! We'll travel light thank you.

I read with Mama tonight and shared some of my journal with her. She always encourages me and makes me feel special. Mama was a teacher for four years before she married Papa, at age twenty-three. She had me when she was twenty-four.

Whenever Mama talks about her years as a teacher, her face lights up. She said it fulfilled her to share her love of learning and to see lights come on inside little minds, to ignite the sense of wonder of all life holds out to us.

Papa didn't go to schools like Mama did. But he loves to read and reads a lot on his own. He says there's lots to be learned from what has passed before so he likes to read history, but also made-up stories. He doesn't share Mama's passion for poems, but he listens when she shares one of her favorites. I guess I inherited Mama's love of words.

Today we had our first Sunday away from home. Everyone on the boat sang hymns together and a preacher read aloud from the Bible. It felt good to acknowledge God in the open-air, magnificent world He created. Back home they're in church missing us as we're out here missing them. I'm peaceful and tired and ready to sleep.

Love, Me

Monday, May 3, 1852

We're coming into Independence, Missouri, today, the gathering place for our wagon train! Then we'll be moving west in earnest and our real journey begins. I still need to write about Papa, Nellie, Burt and my baby sister Elizabeth, who died.

I think I'll have time. Today is Papa.

Papa's name is John and he is tall, like Mama, but stockier in build. He has light brown hair and light blue eyes, the color of the sky in the early morning. I especially love Papa's strong hands and how he uses them to work and play and hold us tight.

Papa teaches me about life, about practical things. I remember the night the cow calved and I got to watch and help. We spent the night on the straw right next to her and dozed to the smell of the horses and the warmth of all the animals inside the barn. Outside, the air was chilly and cold. Papa said he thought that this one might need some help and we should be ready. Sure enough, the little one got stuck as she began to come out.

"Let her be, just a bit," Papa said. "Let's let nature take care of it first, if she can."

And she did, though I held my breath and it seemed to take forever for the baby calf to land on the straw. Whew, what a relief that was. I named her Rose and she's on this journey with us and gives us fresh milk each day.

I've learned so much about nature from Papa. Papa always lived on a farm, so it's natural for him. Mama used to live in the city, before she met Papa. She likes the quiet of the country now.

With growing things, Papa always knew just when care was needed. I'd tag along with him in the fields and he'd talk to me as we went. I had to run to keep up because he has such strong, long legs. My legs are growing now and I'm going to be as tall as Papa, it seems. That's good because it's easier to get onto a horse with long legs.

Papa grew up around horses, so he taught us to ride. He had to teach Mama too. I love to ride. We brought Burt, one of our best horses on this trip. More about Burt, soon.

Everyone is in a flurry about reaching Independence.

Love, Me

Tuesday, May 4, 1852
Dear Carrie,

I remember how lots of people were talking about going west to California and Uncle Peter and Papa sat around the fire talking, and now we're here, ready to begin. Yesterday, we said good-bye to the river and traveled just outside Independence so the oxen could graze on good grass.

We sit and wait, wagons circled, ready to begin our long trek across the country. They say in California there are new towns and good farmland, tall mountains and gold. Papa said it was getting too crowded in the States, too full of people. I hope California is a big place, because from the looks of things here, everyone is going there. I know that isn't possible, it just looks that way right at this moment.

Oh Carrie, so many wagons, thousands of them, as far as the eye can see. The night is ablaze with campfires. I hear fiddling as I sit and write before sleep. The air is filled with celebration. This is our first night camping out on the prairie.

We laid in all the provisions for the trip. We still had loads of flour from home, but they recommend two hundred pounds per adult, so Papa bought more. We carefully put Grandma's eggs into the flour and cornmeal barrels and they keep from breaking that way. We also have about three hundred pounds of bacon, packed in bran, thirty pounds of rice, seventy-five pounds of sugar, twenty pounds of coffee and four pounds of tea, ten pounds of salt, dry beans and dried fruit. We also have saleratus (baking soda), vinegar, and some medicines, including whiskey and rum.

I'm so glad we're light on the furniture because the oxen will have to pull all these staples for us and Papa says they weigh about a thousand pounds. Thank you, oxen.

You should see Nellie. She's such a good old dog. I'm glad she got to come along. She's real excited about all the commotion, the people, dogs, livestock, children, but she minds real well. When Papa tells her to stay, she stays. I guess you figured out that she followed us. Papa gave in and let her come. Now we can't imagine her not being along with us.

Remember how back on the farm, she'd scare away the foxes and coyotes who tried to come in and eat our chickens?

24

She never let those coyotes by. They sure would raise up a ruckus. The coyotes sneaking around, the hens squawking and old Nellie chasing them out.

I guess we call her old Nellie because Papa and Mama had her since before I was born. But no one told her she was old and she doesn't care. She's a real smart dog. It soothes me to have her here with us.

Missing you, miles from home,

Love Katie

P.S. The stars look the same!

My sketch of Nellie

Wednesday, May 5, 1852

Independence seems to have sprung right out of the prairie to furnish emigrants all the necessaries for the trail. Everyone rushes around and you can hear the hammering and banging of the blacksmiths' shops where wagons are being built or fixed and horses and oxen shod.

Papa did all that before we left, so we don't have to pay the high prices here. Some of these men who are going west don't even know how to drive a wagon—that is so hard to imagine. I learned to drive the farm wagon when I was eight. But these wagons are even harder to drive and to control, with the four oxen and being loaded up with all the supplies.

We have to wait for the grass to grow long enough so that there will be enough for all our livestock to eat on the way. With all these people going west on the same trail, I'm not sure how it will work. But Papa says there will be lots of room out there and hopefully, lots of grass.

There's a little girl in our wagon train who looks so much like Elizabeth that I'm missing her sorely right now. I went and talked to Mama and she told me to write about it, so I am.

Elizabeth was my baby sister. She's buried in the church cemetery back home.

Mama says when you really love someone, you never lose them, not even when they die. That's how she felt about her Grandpapa and Elizabeth. She doesn't mean it doesn't hurt. But in some way, you still feel them, their love, their presence. And that helps the pain some.

Elizabeth was so tiny, beautiful and fresh. I didn't think God was fair to take her the way that He did. She loved me, I loved her back and felt her joy.

She didn't have any of the cares of the older folks. I could feel how I was in the middle, between her and being an adult. She lived in the simple joys–watching a butterfly, smelling a flower, smearing peas in her bowl, splashing water in the bath. Even her pain was over fast. She'd laugh right after she cried, and forget the tears. Her light blue eyes, which were just like Papa's, would shine with joy.

I was "Katie," because she couldn't say Kathleen and I wasn't Mama. Sometimes after she was gone, I'd cry about her and feel her snuggled up against me, sleeping like we used to do. I want to stay innocent like that but I don't know how. I'm already feeling myself change. And yet, sometimes, when I think of Elizabeth, I feel that innocence in myself and that nourishes me.

When Elizabeth died, I felt a huge pain in my heart. I was eight and Peter was four. Elizabeth was almost two. The influenza hit her hard and she was gone in two days. There was nothing that Doc Mayfield could do. We held her all that last night, Mama and me taking turns. She was peaceful and beautiful at the end with her blond curls stuck to her forehead.

It was early morning, the dawn just showing over the trees outside the window when she took her last breath. Mama and I cried and held her and each other. Then I rocked her for I don't know how long. I wanted to remember her as the little angel she was. She was just here briefly to remind us of the wonder of life and the gift of love.

I'm sorry, Elizabeth, that we had to leave you behind. I will never forget you. You live in my heart, so in that way you are coming with us. I want to stop here and sleep remembering you. Love, Me

Thursday, May 6, 1852

As we wait for the rest of the train, the oxen graze and fatten up for the trip. I'm glad for that, because once we get rolling, they will have it hard, day after day. I talk to them and tell them that it will all be worth it when we get to California. They'll have lots of open spaces to graze on and, after all, they are making history with us.

I got to ride my horse Burt today, through the open prairie, which flows endlessly on toward the horizon. Riding Burt is a piece of home I bring along, though I ride in new surroundings now. I remember when I first learned to ride. I was five when I first got on Bessie, Burt's mama. Bessie taught me to ride.

It was a long way down from up on her, but I felt her big back under me and she turned to look at me and made a noise with her mouth. Papa said she was saying hello. I said hello back and we were fast friends. I liked her Mama energy right away. She wouldn't think of letting me get hurt and was just as good to Peter when he learned to ride.

Later on, when Peter rode Bessie and I would ride Burt, Bessie would snort at Burt and I think she was telling him to be careful and to not be too frisky, just like a mama would do. Bessie used to like to go along the stream and then we'd get off and let her and Burt rest a bit and get a drink. They'd munch some grass and look around at some new scenery.

Carrie and I rode together, all over the hills, Carrie on Bessie and me on Burt. Sometimes Peter and Carrie's little brother, Paul, would come along and ride behind us. It was glorious. Just the hills, the horses and us. We'd start out early, Saturday mornings, and ride along the forest, by the stream. Spring was my favorite time. We liked to see how many different wildflowers we could gather. We always found new ones. We had over twenty-five different kinds. I have them pressed in a special book at home, with the names written out.

Papa taught Mama and me to ride like a man. He says it is silly for a woman to sit sidesaddle because you control the horse with your legs. He says that someday people will laugh at riding sidesaddle because it is ridiculous, so we may as well be ahead of our time.

I've noticed how people stare at me out here when I ride. I wear special long bloomers under my skirt. When I ride fast on Burt, sometimes I can't tell where he starts and I end. Papa says not to worry about what people think if they see me ride like a man. They don't know what is right. Actually, Papa says not to worry about what people think at all. I love that about Papa.

Again tonight the huge sky blazes yellow with the light from so many fires. Everyone is excited to finally begin our journey west.

Time to sleep out on the open Prairie.

Love, Me

Thursday, May 6, 1852,
Dear Carrie,

Tomorrow I'll be thirteen and a half. I keep waiting to feel different, but mostly I don't. I wonder if it feels different to be grown up. Do you wonder that too?

I want to describe everything to you Carrie just as if you were here. Look through my eyes when you read my words. That way we can still share it, although not in the exact same moment. Mama says that people can be real close through letters. She and Papa were separated for a while before they were married and they wrote each other every day. She says it was a special time in their life and when they knew they really loved each other.

Tomorrow we begin–they say the grass is now tall enough for the livestock. Oh Carrie, I can hardly contain my excitement. But how can I be excited about something I've never done? There are thousands of wagons camped all around, fires lighting up the spring sky, everyone anxious to begin this journey we've all thought about for so long. I've never seen so many people in all my life, yet in the midst of all the crowds, I'm lonely for you.

The fiddling tonight made me think of my last birthday party with you. Remember how Mama made ginger cakes with cream and then we played games and sang? And then Uncle Peter played the fiddle and we danced. I remember crying when I realized it would be my last birthday with you and with everything the same as it had always been. Then I thought I'd better <u>really</u> have fun since it was the last time. Then we laughed and chased and finally all fell asleep in a big heap on the feather bed by the fireplace.

Carrie, do you think we will ever not want to run and play? It is hard to imagine that I would want to sit instead of to run. When I run I feel free.

We were just coming in to our camp last night when the full moon rose like a giant yellow ball and the moonlight glistened on the trees. It seemed so close to the earth, I thought I could ride over and touch it.

I'm starting to write each night just before I go to sleep. The candle shadows dance against the canvas cover of the wagon.

Lots of people die going west, Carrie. I don't want to die. I want to live. I have a lot to learn and say and do. I wonder if everyone feels like that. Guess I'll ask Mama. My heart is brimming with love, laughter and tears all at the same time.
Love, Katie

A quick sketch of our wagon

Friday, May 7, 1852

I sit in our little wagon home, out on the prairie. Today we "jumped off" into the journey to California. They call it "jumping off" I guess because we are leaving behind all civilization for five months of walking across the prairies toward California, so we're "jumping off" the edge of The States.

At dawn, our twenty-two wagons rolled out, all in a line. We traveled all day, covering about fourteen miles and then camped together by a stream, with good grass for the animals. We circled the wagons with each one touching the other and it's a cozy sight out here under the sky. Everything rests quiet now, after so much commotion today. Mama and Papa sleep in the tent, Peter breathes quietly beside me in the wagon. I can't sleep yet for all the energy I feel. My thoughts go back to our last night at home, two weeks ago.

The wagon was ready and we got ready to sleep on the feather bed that would go into the wagon in the morning. I looked at the hearth and the rug, the soft chair where we'd sit evenings and read, the feeling of home which that little house had always meant to me, the only home I'd ever known. We sat together around the fire like we did when Mama would read to all of us.

For months, the trip west was our main subject of conversation. What to take, what to leave behind. Building the wagon, getting it ready, packing, preparing all the provisions, then saying good-bye.

We were leaving at dawn. Everything was ready on the outside. Now, as Mama and Papa said, we needed to take time to get ready on the inside.

We were all touching each other together in front of the fire—me up against Mama, Peter on her other side with Papa next to him. It was good to touch. Our strong family bond made me cry and my tears made the room blurry and my throat choked with emotion.

Papa said, "We're going out there tomorrow and no matter what happens, our family bond of love will bind us, sustain us. God will help us through the hard times. Let us pray together now for guidance, strength and hope for the future." We bowed our heads and all said our silent prayers.

Then we recited the 23rd Psalm together. "The Lord is my shepherd, I shall not want. He maketh me to lie down in green pastures; he leadeth me beside the still waters; he restoreth my soul..." Our voices blended, the sacred words soothed me.

Then Papa looked right into my eyes: "If anything happens to your Mama and me, you go on and make your lives out west. Uncle Peter and Aunt Sarah could help you out till you could make it on your own and you would have each other. God has his own plans and we have to trust his wisdom. I pray that we get there together, but these are words that have to be said."

"I know Papa." I felt his gentle goodness and all my love for him and Mama. We hugged and cried, then Peter made a big snort with his nose and we all laughed and hugged some more.

I carry the memory of that night and of our life before this journey inside of my heart. Tonight, I feel ready to face the unknown. I am thankful we are going together.

Love, Me

Saturday, May 8, 1852

We covered about thirteen miles today. Papa and I keep track. A few muddy spots slowed us down, but we walked the whole day. After the chores and supper, I have a few moments to write. I'm tired. Mama says that as we get stronger, the walking will get easier.

Our wagon is right next to a huge oak tree, so I'm sitting under it and remembering Mrs. Oak back home. Now I sit under a sister oak and watch her light green leaves fill out her graceful form.

Spring. A new season of my life unfolds. I find comfort in the seasons. It makes me realize that I can change, too. I can have gloomy days, sunny days, stormy days. I'm growing a lot right now. My body has a mind of its own. Mama says I'm becoming a young woman and that is special.

I'm not sure about growing up. It looks OK sometimes, but I like being a girl, too. Right now, I'm right in between.

Back home, Mrs. Oak soothed me when I fretted about leaving, growing up or any kind of change. She told me that when you grow, you get deeper roots and stronger limbs and can see farther. That does sound nice.

And as far as going west, Mrs. Oak thought that it was a grand idea. Why, she told me, some of her acorns could go with us and become beautiful oak trees all the way out in California. I thought that was such a great idea that I gathered some up and put them into my handkerchief that very day. They wait safely in my pouch of special things. Mama smiled when I told her about the acorns. We brought seeds with us for lots of things.

The night sky, brimming with stars, sends many shooting across the sky. They feel like kisses. Missing my home.
Love, Me
P.S. I let myself read the first of my letters from Carrie and put it in here.

Acorns from home

33

My Dearest Katie,

It feels odd to be writing you these letters so that you can read them on your journey. And yet you are still here, dear cousin. So I struggle with them, wanting to spend every minute I can with you before you leave.

I want these letters to be a comfort to you, to make you smile, and yet I must admit that I ache with the thought of losing you. But since we always told each other everything, I am going to be honest with you here too.

I don't want to think of life without you. I will no longer be able to skip down the lane and across the field, past sweet Elsie the cow, Rose's mama, past the barn and find you there, meeting me with your warm smile.

My joyful, mischievous, smart cousin who always seemed just a bit larger than life and yet was so much a part of my life that your leaving will open up a huge space that no one else can fill.

Mama told me to start ahead, since I want to write you five different letters. But I couldn't do it, so now I'm writing just before you leave. Mama knows that your leaving will be harder than I can even imagine. And what I am imagining is so hard. I told her today, "Mama, how will I ever be able to manage? I'll just be stuck with a bunch of boys, no girls, no Katie." My dear little brothers are precious to me—but still. She just hugged me and let me cry. That helped some.

I realize that I haven't written letters to you much, except when you went to visit your Grandmama Kathleen that one time for two weeks. I wrote you two letters. But then you were coming right back.

Grandma Josie and I planted the sweet peas together months ago so that I can give them to you in a few days when you leave. I have decided that I'm going to always plant a special flower garden with grandma, in your honor, with all your favorite flowers.

This year, our garden will be cosmos for their soft hues of pink, white, lavender and rose. Zinnias for their bright colors of orange, red, yellow and purple. And sunflowers, for their regal and stately strength and for how they always feel like a friend, or a sister, when they grow so tall, their bright yellow faces turning toward the sun. Remember how we would marvel at how one single seed could create hundreds of seeds so perfectly arranged, spiraling around toward the center?

Mama let me out of some of my chores to write this. The fire crackles and the stew simmers—chicken and vegetables for one of our last special dinners with you. Mama rolls out two pies and will use the berries and sauce we put up last summer. Remember how sweet and juicy those berries were, warmed by the sun, plump and ripe? We'll all share those pies tonight with some fresh cream from Elsie and Rose.

I want to try to think of good things about your leaving because otherwise I just cry. So here is one thing I thought of: We both love words, so I guess it will be special to share just words between us until we can see each other again.

I'm looking forward to our dinner tonight and more memories that I will have to cherish of times spent with you. By the time you read this, we will both be remembering.
Sending you hugs from home and holding you in my heart,
Your cousin Carrie

Sunday, May 9, 1852

I read my first letter from Carrie last night before I went to sleep. I cried and then dreamed about her all night long. Will the ache of missing her ever stop? I don't know and will have to talk to Mama about it.

35

Right now as I write, I watch Mama and Papa and how they work together as such a team. Mama organizes all the cooking. She still makes the best biscuits and they taste so good out here. Papa takes care of the oxen and makes sure the wagon doesn't break down. Peter and I help out.

I remember all the stories Mama told me about when she and Papa met and were courting. Papa would come with a buggy and they'd go for long rides out in the country. Or they'd walk by the river. Mostly they talked. Mama said that right off she knew that she could talk to Papa about anything and he'd listen. Even if they didn't agree, they could talk and listen to each other.

They used to talk about what they wanted out of life, how they wanted to live and how they felt about children and a family. Mama said they had the same feelings in their hearts and so she knew that they could work out everything else.

They both wanted a simple life of love, sharing, laughter and freedom, with wide-open spaces and a place to call their own. I guess that's what is attracting them to the west. Especially the freedom. I can feel the freedom inside me too. It's as if I knew it before and forgot, and it is just on the other side of my memory.

Grandmama and Grandpapa didn't approve of Mama marrying Papa because he was a farmer. They were used to a courtship of parties, balls and formal affairs. But that was not Papa's way.

"You'll just be a work-horse from sun-up till sun-down and all your education will be wasted," Grandmama said.

But Mama loved Papa and married him anyway and things became pretty strained with her parents after that.

Mama has never minded all the work because she and Papa are building a life together. That means something. I notice how they always take the time to show love to each other and say kind words. Papa comes up behind Mama, puts his arms around her and tells her she makes the best biscuits in eight counties and also has the prettiest smile. Mama beams and we all laugh. Or Papa brings her in a special rose he spotted outside. They share love and we feel it.

Out here on this journey, I am especially thankful for Mama and Papa and their love. It gives me my home. Missing Carrie and home.

Rolling and squeaking toward the west.

All love, Me

Wednesday, May 12, 1852

We set out from Independence, Missouri, following the Santa Fe Trail. Today, our sixth day out, we took the right-hand trail and those going to the south of California, took the left. The rain and mud made it slow going and hard on the oxen. We only covered about eight miles.

Poor Tom. He's our lead ox and the strongest of the bunch, and he's pulling so hard. We have to sit in the wagon in an effort to stay dry but still I'm wet and chilled to the bone. I wish for sunlight's sweet face and warm breath on my skin. The gloomy air over the camp weighs heavy on our spirits.

We lost three families who turned back today. They were already homesick, and when they saw the Shawnee Indians running the ferries across the Kansas River, they turned and ran, squealing in sheer fright.

So we're down to nineteen wagons from our original twenty-two. Peter lost a friend and feels sad. I tried to entertain him, though and tickled him to make him laugh. But then Mr. Bret gave him a harmonica and taught him the song 'O Suzanna."

Peter played it for me at least ten times tonight and fell asleep with his harmonica in his hand, probably still playing in his dreams. I do hope he learns another song soon though, bless him.

Sleepy, tired and glad we didn't turn back.

Love, Me

Peter's harmonica

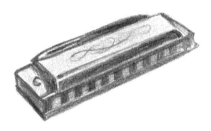

Thursday, May 13, 1852

After the ferry across the Kansas River, things turned so much better. Too bad those families gave up. We're in an emerald sea of grass and more wild flowers than I've ever seen. The animals graze greedily and we stow some grass for the future in burlap bags and use them as pillows to lean on.

Papa and Uncle Peter each made a table of a wood slat, which slides out from under the wagon bed and rests on two poles. It helps to be able to stand to fix meals and to not have to stoop or squat, though the fire still requires stooping. Aunt Sarah really appreciates her table, as she's due to have a baby in about two months.

The high water in the streams from the spring rains makes crossings dangerous and we use Indians crossings whenever we can. Many have drowned. Yesterday, the Bronson brothers were lost in the swift current. Somehow, the wagon and team made it across.

Mrs. Bronson, who lost her husband and brother-in law, sat, stunned as we waited for the rest of the wagons to cross. What to do? Should she try to go on to California with her four children? Tonight, we prayed for her and the others who have lost loved ones.

Love, Me

Friday, May 14, 1852

Dear Carrie,

I'm sitting by a river listening to birds making a laughing sound. Funny new birds I've never heard before. The sound of the rushing water is the same as at home, though, reassuring in its sameness. I remember the stream by the house and the river nearby. How we'd sit for hours and talk and play, and when we were littler, make villages in the sand out of bark and stones and lots of imagination.

I am alone sitting here. Just myself, the water, birds and sky. And of course, the West, more and more West, as far as the eye can see and then more. These waters are new and different, fresh. I've never seen them before. And yet they remind me of our river at home. That's comforting. Yet it's really a mirage, that comfort. These waters are new.

Two days ago, a woman on our train lost her husband and brother-in-law. They drowned in this river when we were crossing over. Everyone feels the tragedy of her loss.

That made me think a lot about the unknown. It seems like we pretend we know what life will bring. We try to make life seem orderly and predictable and routine, like we know what to expect. And yet we don't, really, know what to expect. It's rarely what we think it will be. Did you ever think about that? Maybe I'm thinking more about it because out here we face uncertainty everywhere we turn. And the realization that death can come so fast.

On this journey, living on the edge of the unknown, our only certainty is: We don't know what's ahead. But isn't that always true of life?

Someday you will be able to answer these long letters of mine. Someday I will have an address again. Until then,
Love from your cousin Katie,
Address Unknown

Saturday, May 15, 1852

Wrote to Carrie. I'm not sure my letters will ever even make it back home, but it still feels good to write them. It comforts me to have a connection to something from the past, someone of the past. And yet, I do embrace the future ahead, the unknown. Spent a few hours getting ready to cross a river. There was time to sit and listen to the birds, feel the warm sun, hear the river speak to me. It was reassuring to hear its sounds–quiet, moving, changing, flowing, fresh and new.

We were able to dunk in and wash off. Not an official wash stop, but enough to feel fresher and cleaner. Papa calls us his 'little Injuns' because we're brown from always being covered with dirt. Oh to sit in a hot bath again! The wonder of that.

Peter has a friend and is running around throwing rocks. I'm enjoying the quiet at this moment. Laura and Aurelie are my friends in the train. Laura is fourteen and talks only about the boys. The adults are so busy that sometimes she runs off with one of them alone. I don't want to talk about boys.

Aurelie is twelve and still loves to play with dolls, though she only could bring one tiny one. I like them both, but somehow, I'm in between them and so writing is my friend when I don't have anyone to listen to me.

A girl of fifteen is on her honeymoon in our train. I don't think I'll be ready for marriage for a long time. Mama was twenty-three when she married Papa. Her parents were afraid she'd be an old maid. But she said she knew she had to wait for the right person to come along. And she did. I want to wait too. Papa says I have all the time in the world. That feels good.

Mrs. Bronson, who lost her husband and brother-in-law two days ago, though clearly stricken with grief, has decided to go on to California. Others in the train will come to her aid. One of the teenaged boys from a family will drive her wagon and others help her with the unloading and the oxen. We shared our milk and butter from Rose today and she was grateful.

Nellie rides in the wagon some to rest her poor paws. They're sore from all the miles and miles she has run. But she's excited—she barks and looks around like this is the best adventure she could imagine.

I'm excited and blue all at once today. Excited for the adventure, blue for all the people we left behind. I miss my home. Writing helps me with all the changes.

I read my second letter from Carrie today. So precious to me. I'm putting it in here.

Love, Me

My dearest Katie,

As I write this second letter to you, I'm imagining you reading it as you journey farther and farther west, away from us, away from the life we've known.

Mama suggested that I write about some of my favorite memories with you, the ones I treasure most. And that made me smile, so I'm hoping it will also make you smile when you read this.

41

You have always been my fearless cousin, the one who is not afraid. You are only eight days older than I am, but you seemed so much older to me. I'm the one who would be hanging tight to your back as we'd race along the river on Burt. Or who would be timid about jumping into the lake from the rope swing—even after you showed me ten times how fun it was. You were so right. Once I did it, then it surely was fun.

You have always been there, breaking the trail open ahead of me and I can't imagine how life will be here without you.

I will miss your laugh, dear cousin, and your sense of adventure. Oh Katie, what I haven't told you is that I think it fits for you to be going off into the wild like you are. As much as I will miss you, I'm excited for you to discover the new lands and to tell me about it.

I know that we will see each other again and until then, we can write. Our two worlds will still overlap and our hearts, just from a farther distance.

Sending you love from home, dear cousin,

All my love,

Carrie

Tuesday, May 18, 1852

Dear Carrie,

I awoke this morning with thoughts of you. The letters you tied to the bouquet, five of them, one per week for the first five weeks–I've savored the first two and they've brought me such joy. I just read the second one and you can't know how special it is to read your words. I've laughed, cried and sighed over the letters. They are all worn out from love and reading. I will treasure them always, as I do you.

I'm remembering the last time we saw each other, the morning I left. I will never forget the image of you as our wagon pulled out and I watched you fade into the distance, along with the rest of my life as I had always known it. I carry that image of you in my heart on this journey.

We are in a sea of green grass and it goes forever. The team loves it. We camped for the night along a clean, fresh river. All is quiet, though people talk of Indians nearby. Cholera is killing more people than Indians are, and people are worried. It is some kind of a fever that sweeps through a wagon train and people die within days. Nobody knows how to stop it or what to do for it. Nothing to do but to pray.
All love, from the Prairie,
Katie

Thursday, May 20, 1852
Dear Carrie,

We're on our way to the Platte river, over two hundred miles from the Kansas River. We've been traveling over a week and have almost another week to go. I pass my days walking along behind the wagon, picking wild flowers, pressing some into my journal, enclosing some here for you. You could plant their seeds and have a piece of our journey there with you.

We've settled into a routine now. We rise early and cover ground till noon, rest during the heat and then move on till dusk. We cover twelve to fourteen miles on good days. I feel peaceful, joyful. No one is really tired as yet. I saw an antelope today. They bound joyfully, light on their feet.

Remember Carrie how we'd churn the butter and it would take so long that we'd make up games and take turns to pass the time? Well it's the most amazing thing. Now the wagon churns the butter for me! Every morning, I milk Rose and hang the bucket of cream in the wagon. The wagon churns the butter for me while I walk behind. From all the bobbing and jerking of the

*trail, by noon we have butter and sweet buttermilk. She's such a
good old wagon. She feels as alive as our animals. She's not as
white as she was at the beginning, but I still think she's beautiful
and she is our home.*

Tonight I'm thankful for our wagon home.

Love, Katie

The butter churner

My Dearest Katie,

*I'm here at Grandma Josie's and she is helping me write this
letter to you. We're in her garden and she is tending the sweet
peas and other flowers that are popping up.*

*Grandma and I are talking about your journey and what it
might be like. She's telling me more stories of what it was like to
come to America and leave her home behind in Scotland.*

It makes me think that I have it easy, Katie. You are going off into the unknown while I stay safe behind. That makes me feel less sad for me and more admiration for you.

I'll still have Grandma Josie and Grandpa Graham and all the familiar places and people. It is a good thing you are so adventurous and so strong.

Now we are in Grandma's kitchen—I can hear the clock ticking in the hall and Turnip purrs by the fire. Grandma just baked her apple cookies for you to take with you. I'm nibbling one as I write, yum, still warm. The kitchen smells like apples and cinnamon. I'm sipping hot cocoa with cream and a gentle spring rain patters on the windows. Our flowers will be glad for the watering.

But the rain makes me wonder—how will you manage, sweet cousin, in weather like this and only a wagon to keep you warm? Or will the wagon keep you warm? I hope so.

You are busy packing and we will see you tonight and I am so glad. I'm sorry I had to say that I had a 'special errand to grandma's' so that I couldn't help you. It is hard not to spend every waking moment with you before you leave. But hopefully these captured moments will give you some pleasure out on the prairie.

I promise to write to you and to remember you and to hold you close in my heart. I hope that will comfort you so far from here and from our home.

By the time you read this I will be sending you hugs across the miles and the great prairies,
Love, Your cousin Carrie

Saturday, May 22, 1852

I read Carrie's third letter last night again and smiled and cried. The way she describes being with Grandma Josie makes

45

me feel like I am right there with them, eating the cookies and drinking the cocoa. My heart ached as I looked out of the wagon into the black night sky.

Then, I awoke this morning dreaming of Grandma Josie, Papa's mama, missing her sorely. I could see her, standing by her garden gate, framed by the trellis of baby pink roses she loved so.

She was wearing her blue calico dress, her white apron tied around her petite frame, waving to me, smiling. All the times I'd ever gone over to see her melted together. I was a tiny little one cuddling in her lap, then five, then thirteen and saying goodbye.

Her love enveloped me, as natural as the air I breathed. Grandma always had a smile, a hug, loving words or unspoken approval.

As I remembered her today, I saw her vibrant energy, younger than her years. I saw her throw her head back and laugh, as she did so many times, her brown hair, streaked with gray now, tied back in a bun. I saw her sitting on the porch swing and rocking and holding hands with Grandpa. Oh how she loves Grandpa Graham. They'd talk about the old days, when Papa was a boy and back to when they were children, in Scotland.

I remembered the day we said good-bye. We sat together in her kitchen, holding hands.

Grandma said, "Ah, when we first came to this country, life will never be like that again, Kathleen. Maybe in the west. It was the beginning of a new country. So much hope. Everyone united in the vision of it, simple and pure.

People helped each other. If I was younger, I'd go west with ye."

"Come with us, Grandma, please come," I pleaded.

"No Kathleen, this farm is a part of me. The trees I planted are now tall, strong. Everything here is from my hand, our hands together. It's hard to leave that. When we came here, it was the frontier. Now you're going further west. But you go, go and explore, find the new land and all it has to offer."

"When you write to me, tell me what grows there, the trees, plants and flowers. Tell me what is new and different. You're so good with words, child. I'll love to read your words."

"Thank you, Grandma."

Grandma hugged me close. Suddenly I felt the pain of missing her. We cried together. I could feel her soft body and smell her Grandma smell, a little like her kitchen smells, of cinnamon and apples. She seemed small to me, fragile.

I felt the contrast of my youth and her age, but in the next moment, I felt her strength, the strength of her love, which bound us and would continue to reach across the miles between us.

As if I could read her mind and her heart, I knew how special I was to her, what being a Grandma must feel like and then how hard to be saying good-bye to that special child.

Just then, her cat, Turnip, jumped up, looked at us and began to lick himself in a bored way, like he'd done a thousand times and would do another thousand times. We laughed, glad of the distraction from the pain of leaving.

"I will come back Grandma," I told her.

"I will wait for you child," she replied, wiping her tears with her apron corner.

Now as I think of her, I know that I must go back, I will go back.

I must write to her and tell her about the prairie, the open spaces, so much space. And the land. I know Carrie shares her

47

letters from me also and that makes me see them together in the kitchen reading.

Tired from a long day of walking. Time to sleep,

Love, Me

Sunday, May 23, 1852

Dear Grandma Josie,

We've been gone almost a month and I miss you so and think about you every day. We're out in nature all the time now.

I treasure my memories of the time we spent together in your garden and how you taught me to notice everything going on in nature. It is as if you are present with me here, because as I notice, I can think of you.

You taught me not to be afraid of bees–that they are busy doing their work in flowers and not to interfere with them. I can see the bumblebees diving into the wild poppies in your garden, one after the other, and how we talked about flying that day. How would it feel to fly like a bird or a bumblebee? And the myth about the man who glued on wings with wax and then flew too close to the sun and they melted and he fell.

Do you think, Grandma, that we'll ever be able to fly? Somehow? What a thought that is.

You would love it out here. Every day we walk to a new place and see trees and plants of all kinds. Today I saw lupines, bright blue and so pretty. We've passed oak groves and cedars and pines. There are still lots of wildflowers and we gather wild greens to eat with prairie hen eggs that we find. Those eggs taste more wild than the ones from your sweet chickens. We are still eating those, which we have stowed in the corn meal.

I think of you Grandma when I snuggle under your quilt and pull my warm hat down over my ears and put on my sweater to sleep. All your hand-made gifts keep me warm and cozy and I can feel your love through them. They still smell like the cedar-

lined trunk where we stored them. And I like to think they also smell like you—a hint of lavender soap and cinnamon.

I long to run across the fields to see you again and someday I will.

Sending you all my love from the trail,

Katie.

P.S. I will write again soon.

Tuesday, May 25, 1852

Dear Carrie,

Peter and I got to giggling tonight and couldn't stop, but he's finally asleep next to me in the wagon. I write by the candle hanging from the hickory bow. We had a wild game of hide and seek around the camp earlier, Peter and Aurelie, her brother Romain, Tom, another friend I've made, and me.

Aunt Sarah says it's a wonder we still have energy to play, after walking all day. Guess Grandmama would really think we're really wild now. We are, but it's a pure wild, like the prairie we're passing through.

My friend Aurelie is much more petite than I am. She's delicate, like the French porcelain doll Grandmama gave me, which I left home with you. I feel so strong and sturdy next to her. Papa calls me his little colt because of my long, thin legs and because I'm full of energy and ready to run. Maybe that's why my horse Burt and I get along so well.

The French that Mama has taught us through the years helps me to understand when Aurelie talks with her parents. Whenever I say a few words "correctement," they beam and applaud. I love the game of learning to talk to people in another language by making the sounds that I've learned. Mama talks with Aurelie's parents easily.

The adults always warn us about staying close to camp because Indians may be nearby. I listen, but I'm not afraid.

49

Tonight, while playing, I spotted a wonderful place to hide. It lay just off from camp into the dusk, so I darted over there.

As I stepped into the bushes, I came face to face with an Indian boy, about my age. I froze from the sudden start of finding a human being in a bunch of bushes where I had planned to hide.

If he was startled, he didn't move a muscle. We looked at each other for what seemed the longest time but probably was only seconds. I was breathing heavily from my running, but that was the only sound. He could have been a statue, except I could see his chest raise up with his breath and he did blink once.

During those few moments, I saw goodness and innocence in his eyes. I was a young woman, he a young man. I knew he wouldn't hurt me.

Then he turned and without a sound, disappeared into the night. I stood still, wondering if I'd imagined the whole thing, but I knew I hadn't. Peter came and found me, but after that, I didn't want to play anymore.

I felt moved and confused. Why are we so afraid of Indians? He was just like me. If only people could see that.

I told Mama and Papa what happened and they told Mr. Brown, the leader of our train. They had a watch all night in case of an attack, but I knew there wouldn't be an attack.

Why is life so confusing? Why do we kill each other just because we have different ways?

I miss talking with you and sharing all my thoughts.

Quiet and moved out on the prairie.

Love, Katie

Thursday, May 27, 1852
Dear Carrie,

Oh the troubles we're having. Last night it rained a solid blanket of bugs. Brown bugs covered everything, the wagon cover, the ground. We all slept in the wagon because there seemed to be millions of them. Our oxen became frightened by the mysterious downpour, but the bugs appeared to be harmless and didn't bite. Nellie woofed and snorted, but then settled down between Peter and me.

Tonight, it's hailing, the hail stones the size of lemons. Ouch. I'm staying in. Oh the memory of our dear sweet home does appeal at this moment. Yet one thing I have to say about Mother Nature. She sure can entertain with her variety of unusual tricks. I'm thanking the wagon for keeping us safe.
Wish I could see your sweet face.
All Love, Katie

Friday, May 28, 1852

We passed Fort Kearny, Nebraska Territory, today and stopped to mail our letters. The Fort buildings are made of prairie sod. Unusual, but I could imagine them being a comfortable protection from the elements, especially after our recent bugs and hail.

We're in buffalo country now, they say, and we gather buffalo droppings, called "chips" for fuel, as wood is scarce. They burn fine for our cooking fires.

Haven't seen a buffalo yet, though and I am anxious to see one. We hear stories of stampedes, but Papa says a lot of stories are just that–made up for the entertainment of the speaker and listener, and not to worry.

Thank you, Papa, you always soothe my mind. I want to sketch the Fort and send it back to Carrie but I may not have time. Tired and dirty.
Love, Me

Tuesday, June 1, 1852

We left Fort Kearny and now we're traveling westward, staying close along the south fork of the Platte River, which is about a mile wide. Some say we're entering the real west. Still no trees for firewood, so collecting buffalo chips as I walk along. But the earth smells fresh and rich with spring and the insects buzz around me as I walk along.

We've seen our first prairie dog town. They sit up in their doorways or scamper about and entertain us. We had to wait till afternoon for the river to fall enough, then crossed without incident.

I'm thankful I have my writing to keep me company during times of waiting. That and exploring around make it always interesting.

Love, Me

Thursday, June 3, 1852

Summer feels wonderful. I'm strong and tan and have oh so much energy. Being outside all day is hard on the skin, Mama says, and tries to cover us up, with a bonnet on me and a hat on Peter. I mostly wear it but it gets in the way and sometimes falls down on my back.

"Katie!" I hear, "Put on your bonnet."

"Yes, Mama!" I call back as I run off pulling it back up.

Burt is happy with all the green grass and he makes it possible to ride ahead and scout out the best places to camp for the night. I love to ride him and Mama and Papa aren't afraid, but some of the rest of the travelers have a perfect fit if I ride off, especially alone.

They never believe I'll come back and one woman, Bertha is always calling out when I return: "Land sakes, she's back. Praise the Lord." It's all pretty silly because I'm only riding ahead a few miles. I'm not afraid at all.

Bertha is about twenty-three, so they say. She married at fifteen, has four children and another on the way. It seems like she only knows her own life and is afraid of anyone who's different. I never knew I was different, but being here with lots of other folks, I guess I am a bit different.

We have passed lots of graves from cholera, a dreadful disease which can spread quickly through a wagon train. We hear frightening stories of people being overcome with it and dying in one day and they have to be buried and left behind. Everyone is scared. We pray together every night. Please God, let us make it there together.

Time to sleep. All is quiet except for the howling of wolves. Nellie was barking back at the wolves, but now she has settled down too. The fresh, cool air soothes me.

Love, Me

Burt grazing

Saturday, June 5, 1852

Mama says good writing is telling stories from your head. It's watching the pictures you see and writing them down, just the way you see them. And if you don't tell them, no one else can. They're lost forever. Something about that got my attention. No one else can think my thoughts, about the farm,

Carrie, my life, the West. No one else sees from out behind my eyes, from quite the same angle.

Mama says only people who want to write even think about writing. But if you do think about it, you're supposed to write.

I got behind a bit today, gathering flowers. I couldn't see a human anywhere and the wagons were ahead enough that I couldn't hear them either. For a moment I stopped and stood, alone in that moment and that piece of the West. The silence pressed down hard on my ears.

In the next second, a red-tailed hawk swooped over my head as if to say, "Are you all right?" I laughed and ran ahead, relieved to see the familiar sights of oxen, dust, wagons and people, walking west in the early light.

Mama keeps a journal too. She says someday we'll tell our grandchildren all about our journey and be proud we were pioneers going west to California. I hear the gentle sounds of the camp as it sleeps, the animals grazing, a few dogs barking, the quiet of the west.

Time to sleep.

Love, Me

Monday, June 7, 1852

"Nooning" as we call our midday stop, is one of my favorite times of the day. We stop and rest the animals, let them graze and catch a breath. There are not as many chores to do as the night and morning. At night there's unloading, making the fire, cooking and cleaning up, getting the beds ready, the tent up, unyoking the oxen, feeding and watering for the animals. Mornings are the reverse of nights.

But "noonings" are for resting, feeding ourselves and the animals, and the time feels peaceful. We eat a cold dinner of biscuits and coffee, left over from breakfast, so there's no cooking to do and less clean up.

I usually have a few moments to write, too. At this moment, I sit and gaze at the open prairie. The wagons resemble ships floating in the sea of grass, the wheels hidden in the endless green waves.

Papa says it's good to go slower and really care for our animals—our oxen, our cow Rose and Burt, our horse. The oxen have to pull us two thousand miles over five months and we need to take care of them to do that. Burt gives us the freedom to ride ahead and scope out good camping places. Rose gives us fresh milk and cream every day. Our animals have physical limitations and if we push them too hard, they'll die.

Taking care of them means paying attention. It means finding grass, storing some in the wagon for times when it is scarce, finding good water, letting them set the pace.

The animals seem to sense our states of mind. If we're calm and sure, so are they. The oxen pull strong and slow. Papa says we'll get there just as fast as those who race by us. This isn't a race, it's a journey, and journeys happen step-by-step, day-by-day, moment-by-moment.

We need to do the best we can every day along this journey, then be thankful for what we did, beginning each day fresh. Papa says that's just like the journey of life.

Seems there are many lessons to be learned out on this open prairie and that's one of them.

Love, Me

My Dearest Katie,

Mama has given me some time away from chores again today to work on these letters. She knows how hard they are to write. I still just want to cry and cry.

But I'm going to write about happy times again with you because there are so many. They make me smile and I want you to smile, wherever you are. I'll always remember how we'd bake together and it would be so fun. Just baking biscuits, with you, would have me laughing so hard.

Remember how my baby brothers would want to help, since we seemed to be having so much fun? Then they would end up getting flour all over and that would seem funny too, so we'd laugh some more.

We're planting now, as you know, all the spring crops. I'll miss our times together, looking at the new young green shoots and then, watching the corn grow till it was high enough for us to hide in. Then, in the fall, gathering all the corn, squash and pumpkins together. And making pumpkin pies and jumping in the piles of leaves.

You're going to see so many new things and places and I'll just be here. Oh, if only Mama and Papa would have let me go with you. But they wouldn't hear of it. I'm needed too much here to work and to help out with my brothers and with all the chores. But I so wish I could go with you.

I don't want to think about life without you, but in two days, that will be real.

Some day when I'm grown, I'll come west and see you again. Until then, we'll have to stay close in our hearts and minds.

Love,

Your cousin Carrie,

By the time you read this, I'll be so missing you from here.

Monday, June 7, 1852

Dearest Carrie,

I begin letters to you when we stop mid-day for our noon rest, called "nooning." Then I complete them some evenings or add on like that for days. The act of writing to you helps me to feel *your presence and our bond of love. I ache with missing you right now. I so loved your fourth letter, which I saved until now. I only have one more, but I read them over and over, treasuring your words.*

Remember how we loved to be outside, running and playing? We'd walk for hours or ride to the river or play in the fields, hiding in the tall corn? I can still hear how the corn stalks rustled as we ran through them and can taste the sweetness of the corn when we'd pick an ear and eat it right there. Mama would always have the hardest time getting us to come inside. Day and night, we'd be outside if we could.

Well I <u>live</u> outside now. My home is the outdoors. Only the thin canvas cover of our wagon separates me from nature. I'm outside all the daylong and I feel nurtured by that somehow. The idea of living inside again seems foreign to me right now.

Can you imagine that I walk from sun up to sun down, with just a rest at noon? And I love it.

Oh, there are definitely moments when I miss our cozy log home. Last night it rained and thundered and I clung to Mama inside the wagon, terrified we'd get blown over and drown in the torrents of rain pelting our wagon. The rain soaked through the cover and we got wet to the bone and shivered all the night through.

But mostly I marvel at the joy of living so present to Nature with all her gifts. Warm nights, Peter and I sleep out on the open prairie wrapped in our quilts. The heavens and its canopy of bright stars wink at me while I gather my thoughts to sleep.

When I imagine being inside a house again, it seems that I'd miss so much. The gentle feel of the fresh air all around me, every moment. The smell of the prairie grass when it wears a layer of morning dew. And the sounds. The owl hooting softly to me right now as I write, thunderous crickets, Nellie right next to the wagon, growling and shuffling, the oxen and horses as they rest and feed, fires crackling their last breaths before they die for the night.

The gifts Nature offers are not all pleasant. Alkali dust is something I'll never forget and even the thinking of it makes my stomach turn over. Or even just plain dust, so much dust when I walk behind the wagons. And clouds of mosquitoes, which torment me day and night.

But even with these challenges, I've grown accustomed to the life on the trail. Early up, walking all day, quiet evenings, the company of others. My legs have grown strong, my skin darker.

I do miss baths and I cannot wait to soak for a very long time in the hottest tub of water I can find. I will sprinkle fresh rose petals and lavender flowers in and stay till my skin is shriveled, but oh so clean.

What a wonder to be walking to California. I feel the adventure of each day, embarking on the trail, ending up in a new destination, over and over again. Some places I would gladly live. Others, I am thankful we're hurrying through.

I will never forget these days for all of my life and somehow, I know it is our destiny to be here on this journey. I miss your sweet face.

Hugs and all love,

Katie

Tuesday, June 8, 1852

Every bit of saved weight helps, and every item must do double duty when it can. So Mama uses a medicine bottle as a rolling pin and rolls out biscuits and pies on the wagon seat, which works quite well. Papa chuckles every time he sees her rolling with it and his favorite joke lately has been: "Margaret,

I need another dose of your pastry." His eyes twinkle through his mock seriousness and we all smile. Their joy enlivens our sometimes dreary days and I know that home is our family together. We are content and cozy as we roll along west.

I gathered some flowers resembling sweet peas today and my heart ached for a moment with memories of Carrie, of home. But then I was here again. No, these sweet peas are more wild, as I am more wild. That is how it must be and I'm glad for it. How can I be excited to go to a place I've never been? I don't know, but I am.

I picked a bunch of wild mustard greens and we had a feast of them along with a prairie hen Papa shot. The greens were spicier than those we would raise at home and the hen tasted of the prairie, wild and free. Food tastes ever so good after being outside all day.

Oh to just have a bath. I sorely miss them. Yet I'm a reflection of my wild open spaces. Wild from the wild.
Love, Me

Thursday, June 10, 1852

Another riding story and poor Bertha. Today, when we stopped for our noon rest, I felt restless and wanted so to ride. I just couldn't stomach the cold coffee and bread. The prairie called out to me. I jumped on Burt and at the last moment, called out to Peter to come along. He hopped on behind and off we went.

We rode through the prairie, bright green in the midday sun, open and wide, with nothing for thousands of miles, just some wagon ruts. I let Burt run, with Peter holding tight to my back.

We raced through the high grass, till Peter tugged on my shirt, reminding me to go back, so we turned to head to the camp. For a moment, I thought I'd lost my direction, but then saw our path through the tall grass. Then I heard it.

"Peter, listen. What is that roar?"

"I dunno. C'mon Katie, I'm scared. Let's go."

Burt twitched nervously. We turned and looked. Over the horizon, a cloud of dust and black headed straight at us, hooves pounding.

"Buffalo!" I screamed and dug hard into Burt. He jumped into a run and we rode hard, heads down, the earth trembling behind us, and tore into camp, breathless, barely able to say the word, "Buffalo!"

Papa grabbed his rifle, jumped on Burt, other men followed, riding and shooting up in the air toward the edge of the stampeding herd to make them turn away from our wagons. Women gathered children, holding little ones close and tight.

We huddled together, the thundering roar paralyzing us, trying to breathe through the dust. We didn't know whether to run or stay. I held my breath and stood still, holding onto Peter and Mama.

We had all heard stories of buffalo stampedes, which had wiped out whole wagon trains. I prayed: "Please, buffalo, just go by us, don't run over us."

Shots rang out, men yelled, the buffalo came closer. I could feel the heat of their masses and smell their sweat. As I peeked out from Mama's shoulder, I saw thousands of buffalo stampeding, right alongside our camp. Not, thank you Lord, *through* it.

The men had headed off the herd, shooting and calling and the buffalo had veered slightly, a few feet. That variance saved our train. Some of our own cattle ran off, but we found them later this afternoon. Rose didn't budge, God bless her.

The riders shot some cows and we celebrated tonight with milk, meat and marrow. And thanksgiving for our lives. We ended up staying put the rest of the day, with the work from the butchering and the gathering up of the livestock and drying some meat for other days. Nellie liked the buffalo meat as much as the rest of us.

Tomorrow we will begin again. The preacher says it was an omen from God that we will be blessed on our journey.

Peter and I didn't get scolded for riding out. But I could feel Bertha's disapproval, like she wanted to blame me for the buffalo. Truth was, the few moments of warning we provided could have been the saving grace.

I will never, in all my days, forget the sight, sound and smell of so much life moving in one direction. Frightening, awesome and wild. I'm tired and comfortable in my quilt made by Grandma. It feels like being held in her sweet arms after such a powerful day.

Thinking of her out here in the wild, wild west.

Love, Me

Buffalo

Friday, June 11, 1852

We're on our way now to Fort Laramie, in the Territory of Wyoming. I listen each night as Papa and the men discuss how far we've come, how far to go and the next big landmark to cross. Papa's practical wisdom has gained the respect of the whole train and people value his opinions.

I'm proud of Papa. He also knows how to use a gun, a skill that many of the other men don't share. Mr. Green shot off his gun accidentally today and just missed his foot. Papa says we face more danger from those firearms in unskilled hands than we do from any Indians.

Now the endless green grass has turned to green-brown, but the oxen don't seem to mind the brown grass. I love the dry weather, remembering those first few shivering nights of cold.

We're in sight of "Court House Rock". I must try to sketch it. It's fun to find things from our guidebook. It feels like a treasure hunt and reassures us that we are progressing on what seems, at times, like an endless journey.

Doing lessons at night with Mama gives me comfort. Learning more French. *Bonsoir.*

Love, Me

Saturday, June 12, 1852

We had to get up and travel for miles so that the cattle could feed, so breakfasted late while they grazed. Now we have good water and grass. Chimney Rock stands out through the clear morning light, rising up out of the prairie. So called, I guess, because it well resembles a chimney. I have to pause now because we're starting off again.

Evening

We passed by Chimney Rock and were able to climb up a ways and carve our names. So many thousands before us have done the same. I wonder at the fate of these pioneers who have gone before us. Will I ever come back and read my name again? Maybe Carrie will someday cross these plains and see my name. Those were my thoughts as I left behind my initials: K.M.McC. 1852.

A light rain settled down the dust as we walked into the twilight. Papa had ridden ahead and found us a fine camp with water and grass. High bluffs surround us now. The area is called Scotts Bluff. From the high ridges, we can see Laramie's Peak far in the distance.

Chimney Rock

Sunday, June 13, 1852

We're spending the morning resting and letting the cattle feed and in honor of the Sabbath. We'll travel later, after the heat of the day has passed. They figure we have a couple of weeks left to get to Fort Laramie.

We're in Sioux country now. The guidebook tells us they are very dangerous. A small party came into our camp this morning. Their horses were the finest I've ever seen. Mr. Brown and Papa talked with them. They wanted to trade with us for some of our flour, but we can't spare any. We traded some clothing for moccasins. I'm so excited to have my own pair of moccasins. They feel soft and soothing to my poor tired feet.

The Sioux women rode with tremendous grace and ease. I thought them lovely, sitting astride their ponies, watching us so intently. They wore beaded skins, their hair flew long and wild, and I imagined them to be princesses, come to visit me on my way west. I will never forget them and would hope to someday ride with such strength and beauty.

Love, Me

Monday, June 14, 1852

We passed by the Sioux encampment today. Mr. Levitt, who travels with his wife and son, knows some Sioux. He introduced Bull Tail, their chief, and translated for Papa, Mr. Brown and some of the men as they traded. Peter stood with Papa.

Our train stood on one side of the stream, their encampment on the other. They lined up to stare at us, as we did them, the men in front, the women and children behind, as our two worlds overlapped. How strange we must have appeared to them, wearing so many clothes, rolling along with wagons filled with possessions, to an unknown destination months ahead, on the other side of the great mountains.

I looked at their village. Their lodges, maybe two hundred of them, built of skins and reeds, smoke circling out of the tops, lined neatly on the ridge above the stream. Young boys helped with the horses–more horses than I have ever beheld in one place. Papa says there were near two thousand of them, wild, fresh horses, as wild and free as these Sioux.

Young women gathering wood near the stream stopped their laughing and conversing to gaze at us. Children ran to older sisters, aunties, mamas and waited. Then Bull Tail stood at the edge of the stream and greeted us. He stood regal and tall, his deep rich voice filling the space between us as he prayed and raised his hands and face to the sky.

As Mr. Levitt translated, I remember the words "Oh Great Spirit" and found myself enjoying the sound of Bull Tail's words, even when I didn't know what they meant.

After the trading was done, the chief touched Peter's arm, looked at Papa's light eyes and exclaimed. Then he walked into our group and pointed at my reddish/brown hair and my green eyes. He became very agitated when he spotted fair little Lucy Barnes and her mama, moved toward them and stopped.

He spoke to Lucy in his Indian tongue. For a moment, everyone froze, especially her mama. I flashed on all the stories I'd heard of Indians taking children, especially the blonde ones. But in that instant, I knew this man would not do that. When he passed in front of me, I had looked into his eyes and saw just empty sky and behind that, love.

Then Lucy thrust her arms out to him, a gesture of innocence and trust. He picked her up and threw back his head in such pure laughter and delight that Lucy giggled too. The tension broke and everyone relaxed.

He was a Grandpa, she a child. Love was present. Mrs. Barnes was visibly moved and I felt the same recognition of goodness, which I felt the night I encountered my young Indian. Only today, everyone felt it.

These people want to live and be free, just as we do. They are no different from us except for the destiny which made them live on these plains, which we pass through.

I long to learn their ways, their language. I feel their heart and love and I will carry that with me to my new home far away. I will never forget this day.

Love, Me

Tuesday, June 15, 1852
Dear Carrie,

So much happening on the outside and the inside, too. We're traveling through Sioux territory and camped near a Sioux encampment last night. We traded some horses with them and things went so well that we decided to camp for the night near them. Their chief came to our camp in the evening and gave us special gifts of dried buffalo meat and moccasins. We were all moved by the powerful goodness of this man and his people.

Oh, you would have been a star today with your light hair and eyes–they haven't seen that, their own features being dark, and they find it fascinating to behold.

The ponies we received from them are full of spirit and energy. Tom's family traded for one and he allowed me to ride her. She's a brown speckled mare, petite, but oh so gentle and strong. The Indian horses remind me of the Sioux themselves–powerful, wild and free, yet calm. Tom and I rode out today to scout a camp. Burt has even become more alive and spirited since the Indian horses arrived.

So much to learn about life. How narrowly we live, assuming we have the only way. Oh Carrie, I know back home people tell dreadful stories of Indians. But they cannot be true. What a gift to meet them and to discover that underneath we are all the same.

I am filled with hope and love and sending it home to you.
All Love, Katie.

Sioux young woman

Friday, June 25, 1852

Reached Fort Laramie and posted my letters back home. No letters for us, but then how could they have beaten us here? Oh, to receive a letter again someday, especially from Carrie or Grandma.

The only real letters I received before were from Grandmama and they were so stiff and formal. I never knew what to write back because everything I'd think of to say, she'd disapprove of. So Mama and I would labor over those together. I'd tell her about my reading and schoolwork and my handstitching and how tall I'd gotten. She liked that. I could also tell her about our cats, because she has a beloved cat, Shakespeare.

But someday I will receive a letter from Carrie. I trust that. Maybe some are in saddlebags somewhere crossing the plains at this very moment. The trapper who carried off my letter today had his saddlebags bulging with letters home.

The buildings of the Fort are made of adobe or sun-dried bricks. Papa couldn't get over that, so we studied them for a time. We talked to a few fur traders, then passed on to encamp at the river about four miles out. Good water and grass for the oxen, Burt and Rose.

Love, Me

Dearest Katie,

This is my last of the five letters and I'm hoping that you'll be reading it far, far from home. In other words, I'm hoping that you are traveling safely and well on your way to California. We'll be looking at the maps and wondering where you are by now.

I've been thinking about you as I lay in my cozy bed these nights before you are to leave. By now you've been sleeping outside on the ground or in the wagon for almost six weeks. Everything in my life here is so familiar and safe and for you, nothing is at all familiar and safe.

I've talked to Mama and Grandma Josie about it and Grandma says that it takes a group of courageous people to open up a new land and that is what you are doing. And Mama says that she is grateful that we're not going. But then maybe I shouldn't tell you that. I do see how your Mama and Papa really want to go and so does Uncle Peter. So that makes a difference.

This last letter has a set of jacks for you to play with and to remember how much fun we had playing together for hours and hours. I was thinking too of all the other games that you can

68

play on your journey that we have played together. Tag, hide and seek, hop scotch, to name a few and I'm hoping that you are finding friends to play with. But then maybe you don't have time to play on your journey?

You are so special to me dear Katie and I will never forget you.

I'm sending you love from here across the miles and miles between us,
Your cousin, Carrie

Saturday, June 26, 1852

I just read Carrie's last letter. I saved it nineteen days after the last one because I wanted to have one more letter to look forward to. I don't know when I will next be able to read her sweet words in a new letter.

She gave me a set of jacks and I will try to teach Aurelie how to play when we get somewhere with a flat and hard place to bounce the ball. No time to write today as we're traveling far and fast due to good weather.

Sunday, June 27, 1852

Papa says we've traveled about 635 miles so far in our two-month's journey, almost 1/3 of the trip. Now we're traveling along the North Fork of the Platte River. We're passing through the Black Hills, which are full of pines and cedars, so wood is plentiful. The days stretch out, long and uneventful. I love the fragrance of the pine trees, their cones and boughs reminding me of Christmas. And the cedars smell sweet and clean.

I wish I could write and walk, but can't figure out how to do that. So I think and walk and then, first chance I get, nooning or bed time, I write it all down. Some nights, I'm bursting with all the news of the day, all the thoughts and events. I remember our Sioux friends with love and sometimes think it was all a dream.

I feel a deep longing, for what I do not know, as I sit under the open sky.

Ready to sleep.

Love, Me

Monday, June 28, 1852

We had to leave the river and climb hills now, but still wood and shade are plentiful. These long quiet days, I find myself thinking back to home, goodbyes and feel the emptiness again of leaving behind loved ones. Earlier today, I felt excited. Writing might help.

I remember the night last November as I helped Papa arch the hickory branches over the new sturdy wagon we'd just built. The autumn moon rose just above the horizon and slanted into the barn door and added to the soft lantern light, which lit up the familiar old space. At that moment, I felt the powerful ache I feel now, of leaving my home behind.

"Papa, why *are* we going to California? Some days I'm excited and others I can't imagine leaving. Right now, I'm sad about it all." I muttered, my voice cracking.

Papa stopped his work, turned to me and studied my face for a moment. Then he spoke, looking at me, softly.

"We have a good life here. But the frontier, Katie, the end of this huge country, as far west as you can go. That calls to me. The land is rich for farming, the winters are mild, it's a new territory and the chance to be among the first to settle it. We'll make our home there. I want it for all of us, for you and for your children's children."

"But Grandma and Grandpa?" I pleaded.

"Yes, I know. It breaks my heart, too, to leave them. But they could come out later, when it's not so hard."

Remembering that night and home fills me with memories of Grandma. I long to see her and yet I feel her here with me now, as I write. She made me all my special gifts. The quilt I sleep in

70

now, the pillowcase with my name tatted in pink letters, "Kathleen." I learned to spell my name by feeling those letters. And a warm wool cap and mittens, socks and a sweater, which have warmed me through the cold times.

When you have to leave behind all your possessions, it gives you pause. You can see the real value of things. And all Grandma's gifts came along with me, contribute to my survival, surround me with love.

Time to add a few words to my letter to Carrie. Somewhat less blue.

Love, Me

Grandma's quilt

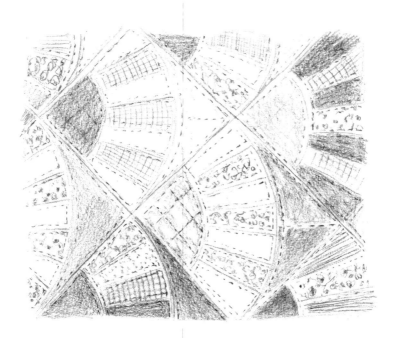

Monday, June 28, 1852
Dear Carrie,

Oh Carrie, please hug Grandma for me and tell her how I miss her and how well her gifts serve me out here on this journey. Someday I'll have a room again with my quilt high up off the ground on a warm feather bed. But tonight I make my bed right on Mother Nature and Grandma's quilt wraps me with love. I will write more later.

All my love from the west, for now,
Your cousin Katie

Thursday, July 1, 1852

We built a ferry to cross the Platte River at the upper crossing. All crossed safely, except the Thompsons lost their cow. I went and hugged our cow Rose and had a conversation with her.

"You're too smart to drown, aren't you? You're coming with us so you can be a mama cow out in California. Someday you'll have a warm barn again, but right now, this is exciting, isn't it?" She mooed and blinked.

Every morning and evening when I milk her, I pat her, hug her and thank her for her milk. She supplies milk for us, Uncle Peter, Aunt Sarah and their boys. Sometimes Mama exchanges milk for other supplies. One family, the Gilberts, have two laying hens, so we get fresh eggs for some of Rose's milk and cream. We've used up all Grandma's eggs by now. We're almost to Independence Rock. It looks like a big whale sitting out on the prairie.

There's fiddling tonight, in honor of the fourth of July being tomorrow. Everyone is excited to celebrate Independence Day so far west.

Love, Me

Rose

Sunday, July 4, 1852

We reached Independence Rock and had a fine celebration. We recited what we could remember of the Declaration of Independence and sang some patriotic songs. Then, it being Sunday, we sang some hymns and the preacher gave a sermon about the value of patriotism, and being true to God and one's country.

We nooned at the rock, then pushed on. We have to keep going because there's Alkali water here or no water at all. The poor cattle. We can't let them drink it or they die and they try to get to the water, so we hurry on through.

We passed many dead oxen and lost one from our train. Mama gave Rose a dose of whiskey and lard after she drank some of the bad water and she came out of it, but it scared me so. In the dry salt lakes, I scraped up some saleratus (baking soda) for biscuits.

Peter and Aurelie and I climbed to the top of Independence rock. The view of the valley of the Sweetwater River down below, and to the west, the mountains rising up out of the plains, the openness and freedom, it took my breath away.

Peter and I stood and hugged and shivered together at the prospect of our future laid out before us. At least that's what I was thinking. I'm not sure what was in his mind. But it was a moment I will never forget on this journey west.

Toward sundown, we came to the Devil's Gate. Here the river cut sheer walls with high cliffs on either side and spilled over to a drop of four hundred feet below. Peter and I stood and looked over and again held onto each other from the thrill of all that water crashing down.

Luckily, the wagons passed through another way. We stopped to camp with good water and grass, so the teams are happy. I'm peaceful and clean from a dip in the river.

Time to sleep.

Love, Me

Monday, July 5, 1852

This valley of the Sweetwater gives us hope and refreshment on our journey. The long drives and dry weather have begun to show on the cattle. Papa says we should slow down a bit here and allow them to fatten up for the last half of the trail. We have grass to their knees and sweet, clear water, so we allow them long noon rests and free roam at night. We're making good time and I feel the strength of knowing we're half way there.

I look out at the circle of wagons, the smoldering fires. Somewhere out on the prairie, antelope and buffalo graze. At this moment, I'm glad about my life. Peter and I sleep out under the sky, Mama and Papa in the wagon. I write by a candle and look up at the night sky.

At home, Carrie could be looking at the same stars. That thought comforts me. It means we're linked by the sky, the same stars looking down on us.

This is my first private journal that is bound like a book. It is fun to be writing a book. I'd like to write lots of books someday.
Love, Me

Tuesday, July 6, 1852
    We're on our way to the south pass of the Rocky Mountains. We go over our guidebook each night to mark our progress toward the next landmark. The guide tells us that it will take five to seven days to travel the one hundred miles to the pass.
    Though we're in the middle of the Rocky Mountains now, with high peaks and ridges all around, the valley of the Sweetwater guides us along, with water, grass and easy grades. We can hardly tell we're going up, though the nights are cold. Mama and I read before bed. Peter progresses with the harmonica and knows five new songs and is very proud. A baby was born today, a little girl. We pushed on after a long nooning. The sweet cry of new life. Such joy.
Love, Me

Rocky Mountains

Wednesday, July 7, 1852

Dear Carrie,

We travel up the Rocky Mountains, but the valley of the Sweetwater River takes us up gently and easily. We have good water and grass for the oxen and they are greatly benefiting from the gradual ascent.

Oh Carrie, I am about to go over the pass where the water will start to flow west, down to the Pacific. Before, I could watch the waters flowing and know they were all flowing back toward you. Soon, they will be headed toward the Pacific, that great body of water, which I hope someday to see.

Mama and I found some mint plants and loads of gooseberries down by the river and what a treat. We made Mint tea and gooseberry tarts and surprised Papa and Peter. We gave some to Uncle Peter and Aunt Sarah, too. Aunt Sarah will have her baby before long and the days are hard on her. She seemed to perk up with the tart and especially the tea.

We passed the famous Ice Slough and Papa dug down to a layer of ice, through the muck. Strange to see.

We're still in Sioux territory, though there are rumors of Crows, Blackfeet or Snake War parties. Several trains have had cholera and we pass new graves every day. I pray with thanksgiving for our safety. I miss you and send you kisses.

Love, Katie

Thursday, July 8, 1852

It feels like the height of summer now, though there's snow on the Wind River Mountains to the north. The high elevation gives us wildflowers, which are such a delight. There's ice on the water bucket in the morning. The clear air and few trees make things appear closer that they are. We look out over a

76

broad, treeless valley for twenty to thirty miles. Want to write to Carrie.

Love, Me

My bouquet of wildflowers for Mama

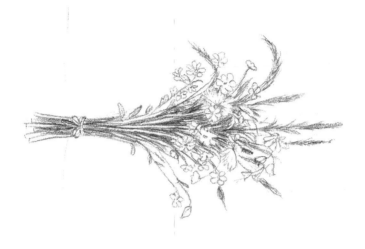

Thursday, July 8, 1852

Dear Carrie,

The wildflowers remind me of you and of our many springs together. We're high up in the mountains where it is just now spring, so I get to have my favorite season twice this year.

If you could just see the flowers. So lovely–purple and yellow, blue and orange. Bright and soft at the same time, mixed with the greens and the browns of the earth. I want to paint that someday, so I sketched it in my journal and I'm letting the image soak deep into my mind so I can remember it just the way it is today.

Some of the flowers are dainty and delicate, like the pink wild roses I found today. They remind me of home and especially of Grandma. Others are strong and vibrant, deep purple lupines, bright orange poppies. I was thinking Carrie, that if they could talk, they'd have different voices, different messages to give us, lessons to teach us. As I gathered them today, I listened for their wisdom.

The poppies look so delicate, yet their roots dig down deep to find water and can survive where most others couldn't. They would tell me to plant myself and dig down deep.

The wild roses would tell me to find a place where I can climb and spread out, a place with lots of room to grow and not to be afraid to become tangled up with others.

I stood still and was quiet so that I could imagine hearing them. Mama called out to me to not lag behind, but when she saw me gathering flowers, she just smiled. I can't imagine getting lost out here, but it has happened. Just last week, little Lucy Barnes got left behind and we thought we'd lost her for good.

When we started out, her Mama thought she was in another wagon, with her Auntie. But at nooning, she was nowhere to be found. A party of riders went back and we waited an extra hour before pushing on. We all said a prayer for her. I sensed that she was all right, and I told Mama, but I didn't tell anyone else. You can't explain those things that you just know.

Luckily, a wagon train about an hour behind us heard her crying and saw her sitting all alone in the long grass. They picked her up and brought her in at dusk, with the riders just ahead of them. What a panic for her Mama until she arrived! And what a joy when she came riding into camp in a wagon full of strangers. It was a moment of pioneers helping pioneers, of strangers becoming kin.

The wagons which brought her in camped with us and may be joining up with us. After supper and a prayer of thanksgiving, we had fiddling and dancing to celebrate her safe return.

Tonight, I sat a little away from the music and watched the moon. An owl hooted, punctuating my thoughts. I am learning to trust and notice those times when there is something worthy to see, or something to hear in my heart.

I sat still and waited. A fawn came up on my left and stood, listening and noticing, just as I was. As the moon shone her light on us, she saw a young woman and a young deer, both wondering at their world, sharing one moment in the immense universe of moments, which make up a life.

And then, as silently as she appeared, my fawn sister disappeared back into the thick folds of the night.
Quiet, sleepy and missing you dear cousin,
Love, Katie

Friday, July 9, 1852

The train has stopped because of cholera. So many people are sick. I'm scared. I don't know what I'd do if I lost anyone out here, alone. Mama looks pale and is resting and I'm getting a dark feeling of dread and fear. Papa cares for her and says he's strong and can withstand it. I don't know. We buried five people today and had to burn their belongings so others don't catch the disease. Sorrow hangs over our camp, so high in the mountains. Tired and uneasy.
Me

Saturday, July 10, 1852

I am so worried now. Both Mama and Papa are sick. Uncle Peter says I can't go to see them because I could catch this terrible disease, but I am going to go anyway.

How can this possibly be happening to us? Where is God? My brother is crying and shivering and I have to try to help him.

Late Saturday night

I can't write because my tears are wetting the page, but I am going to try. I just want to scream and howl but I can't.

I lost both of my parents today, killed by cholera.

I stare at those flat and empty words, which mean that my whole life and existence are gone.

Mama told me to write about all of life, the joy and the sorrows. That writing could help me to understand my life. I promised I would.

I write now just to keep my promise. I am angry and I can hardly see through my tears. I'm doing this for you, Mama.

When I went to see her, she held my hand and looked deep into my eyes. I put my head on her chest and sobbed. She spoke softly, slowly.

"Shhh, shhh, Katie, it's all right. God has His plan. We don't always know why He works the way He does."

"Don't go Mama. I can't lose you. Don't go."

"If I go, there's a reason. Something neither of us will understand, maybe not until the end of life. But you have to trust, Katie and stay in your heart. Keep your heart open, even in the pain."

She was whispering now and the look in her eyes seemed to be farther away, like she was seeing something besides me.

"I love you sweet Katie. I don't want to go, but it seems I'm being called. Stay strong, Katie. Stay..." and then she stopped and I could feel the life in her fading away.

"No. No. No." That's all I could scream out through clenched teeth and silent sobs. I wanted to shriek and cry and strike out, but I couldn't move.

I kept my head on her chest, the chest I'd spent so many years up against, wanting to remember every detail of her sweetness and her, just her. She was gone but I could pretend for just a little while and hold onto her.

Peter came in. I held him close and he knew before I said a word. "She's gone." is all I said. We held each other and Mama, crying together. When Uncle Peter came in, he made us let go. In a real gentle voice he said:

"I'm so sorry about your Mama. But you best be careful about catching the cholera yourselves. Best to let go now. Go see your Papa. He's real bad."

So like a couple of sleepwalkers in a nightmare, Peter and I stumbled over to be with Papa. He died within a few hours of Mama. I sat with him like I did with Mama. Peter fell asleep with his head in my lap.

Papa didn't say much, but that was his way. I looked into his light eyes, held his big, rough hands in mine. He was so stocky and strong. I thought about his gentle nature and yet how he could stand his ground. Papa knew what to say and when to say it and people listened when he spoke. He was wise and able and always knew how to fix things.

Then why was this happening to him? I tried to be strong for him, but I just couldn't.

Just before he died, I hugged him and cried and he stroked my hair. Peter woke up and clung to both of us and was clearly frightened. I was numb. All I could think of was, Please God, let me wake up to a bad dream and be back in our cozy home before we left. Please God, don't let Papa die, too.

Papa sensed the flow of life and nature, life and death. But why God, why Papa? I don't understand.

Papa seemed really peaceful at the end. Uncle Peter led us away to scrub all over with lye soap and burn our clothes. Then he put us to bed in our wagon. I'm wearing some of Mama's clothes from the trunk right now. I can smell her and feel her and I can't believe she's gone.

Both Peter and I are in a daze. He's asleep beside me but I can't sleep. I had to write. It's all I can think of to do right now except to cry.

Peter is fitful and I want to comfort him. My heart aches. I am angry at God. Please help me to understand. My heart feels torn open.

Love, Me

Sunday, July 11, 1852

I can't see where we are and what is happening around me. I feel lost inside a world of sorrow. People seem to understand and are letting us alone. Hans, a teenaged boy from a Danish family offered to drive the wagon for Peter and me, till I can do it. I'm grateful for the help.

We lost almost half of our train to the cholera and so many others are as devastated as Peter and me. It swept through our train like a wind over the prairie. Some died within hours, some lasted a day.

Life. Beautiful Mama lying there but no life in her. How can that be? Just hours before we were laughing in the sun, hugging goodnight, telling stories by the fire, talking about how it would be when we were west and had our warm house and our cozy library with all the books we could ever read and then some.

Papa, you were always so strong, never sick. I don't understand. Why didn't we all just die? Peter and I are lost without you. Mama, how could you leave and not ever see the west? That was your dream.

"God works in His own ways," was the answer I felt in my heart.

Tonight as I lay awake trying to sleep, I prayed to understand God's ways. They don't make any sense to me at all right now. I wish so to go back and have it all be a bad dream. But every moment, I remember that it isn't a dream and with a heavy heart I try to sleep. Nellie is a comfort as she sleeps at my feet.

Love, Me

Monday, July 12, 1852

Peter seems to need me a lot these days. He walks alongside me and doesn't want to be with his friends. We talk and that is good. Today we had a real sweet talk.

He cried and told me how he couldn't stop feeling afraid.

"They're gone, Peter. I don't understand either. It's terrible and I'm so sorry," I said, and stopped and held him for a moment.

Peter sniffled and sobbed. "I just can't. I can't get used to it."

"I know, I know. My heart is broken open, just like yours. There's no way I can even imagine life without Mama and Papa, no way," I told him. I rocked him gently as I hugged him, feeling his slender young body. Holding him like that, I suddenly felt much older than thirteen years.

"They're still here with us. We just can't see them or touch them. But we can still think about what we would tell them, what we would laugh about. What would they think about where we are today? Now you think about that and when I tuck you in tonight, we'll talk some more."

He seemed to feel a little better and ran off to ride in the wagon with his friend Abe.

Tonight as I said goodnight to him, he said:

"Do you think we'll be all right in the west without 'em Katie? What are we gonna do?"

"We'll be all right, Peter. Remember the last night at home, before we left, how we all held hands and prayed? Papa said if something happened to any of us, that whoever was left had to go on for the sake of all of us."

Peter looked up at me. "Yes, I remember. But oh, I never thought it would happen, not to us, not to Papa or Mama."

"Yes I know. Neither did I. But it has and we will go on. We have each other now, don't we? And we'll go on for them."

He'd stopped crying, but the tears stained his dusty cheeks. He managed a half smile. "Yeah."

"We have everything they taught us, all the love we shared. Peter, somehow we'll get through this."

"Yeah, I guess so."

"Now we'll read and tell stories, just like we always did."

"All right. Katie, I don't know what I'd do if I didn't have you." He looked like he was going to cry again.

"Well you do have me, and you're stuck with me, in fact. Now let's get to those stories before it gets too late."

I am finding my strength. I have to go on for Peter, for myself and of course for Mama and Papa. I'm not sure how, but in this moment, I know I must do that.
Love, Me

Tuesday, July 13, 1852
Dear Carrie,

It's been three days since Mama and Papa died. My heart still aches so I can't see straight. Nighttime has been the worst time. Peter and I huddle together in our wagon, next to Aunt Sarah and Uncle Peter's. We cry and talk about how much we miss them. Aunt Sarah says I should be strong for Peter, and I try, but Mama always said to feel, so I am.

Peter really needs to cry too. Sometimes I think grown-ups are too cut off from their feelings and life. After a while it seems like they don't feel anything anymore, good or bad. Like when Aunt Sarah sets her mouth real tight and says to hush up about Mama and Papa. At least Peter and I have each other.

We talk about what we miss and what we'd say and what they'd say back. We whisper so Aunt Sarah won't hear or she'd say: "Crying won't bring them back." I know that is true, but we can't help it so we go on as best as we can. Uncle Peter is really sweet and doesn't say much. He lost his brother when Papa died, so I know he's hurting, too. He understands.

I like to remember Mama brushing my hair at night and our special time to talk. Seems like that's when we would talk about private things. Mama always listened and understood. If I talked about growing up, she'd say that I didn't have to worry. Time would take care of it and I'd really love being a woman. Right now, I could just be right in between. That's surely where I am.

With Peter, I'm just his sister who loves him and can comfort him some, but I guess the womanly part helps. I miss feeling Mama's warmth as she would hug me. That's what I want to remember. I don't think Mama had a hurting thought in her mind and I know she's with God in heaven now.

Of course, Papa is there with her. At least they are together. They taught me so much about love just by watching them. They had their differences, but would reach out to each other, hold a hand, take a moment and just be together.

It was like what they were doing in life together was the most important. They both had such big hearts and their hearts would win out over their minds, it seemed. I never saw them stay angry for long.

Mama told me: "You're going to be a fine woman, Katie. You have a way with words and that's a gift. You follow that. It's a blessing to know how to read and write and to share that joy with others." Mama was right. I do feel better when I write and that's a gift to me. I won't let her down.

I feel her nearby. She didn't want to go. I can't imagine life in the west without her. But then I can't imagine life without her at all. Aunt Sarah says it will feel better over time. I know that was true with losing Elizabeth.

But now, Peter and I just hope she's right. I miss Papa too, but night times were my time with Mama, so I guess I think of her most now. Daytimes I think of Papa.

The west is a lonely place at night when you're all alone. In my heart I know I'm not alone. But I still fall asleep on Grandma's pillowcase wet with tears.

All love, your cousin

Katie

Wednesday, July 14, 1852

I so miss Mama and Papa. I guess I always will. The day Elizabeth died, I had Mama there to help me through. I always had Mama to help me through. I can't believe I lost them both. Yet the days go on and they don't come back.

We had to leave them back on the trail and cover over their graves with dirt and run the wagons over and over to make sure the coyotes, wolves or Indians didn't dig them up. That's a horrifying thought, but it has happened and then the Indians get the cholera from the clothes and things they take. We also had to burn uncle Peter's tent, since papa died in there, and the bedding mama died on.

Papa would be fine lying in the earth like he was, just a thin sheet around him. We buried them together, just like they were in life, side-by-side, loving each other and going forth together into unknown territory, just like we are.

We sang two hymns, one for each of them. "Blest be the tie that binds" was for Mama.

Blest be the tie that binds
Our hearts in Christian love;
The fellowship of kindred minds
Is like to that above.

We sang "Joyful, Joyful we adore thee" for Papa.

Joyful, joyful we adore thee
God of glory, Lord of love;
Hearts unfold like flowers before Thee,
Hail Thee as the sun above...

I chose the hymns but I couldn't sing through my tears. So I just thought the words in my heart. We ended with the 23rd Psalm.

"The Lord is my shepherd, I shall not want. He makes me lie down in green pastures; he leads me beside still waters; he restores my soul..."

Then I really cried, remembering our last night at home and how we prayed together. Now I see that Papa's words were prophetic. Could he have known somehow and had to prepare us?

We had a lot of courage, I think, as I look back now and see our family together in our cozy home. We had a good life by many standards. We had a prosperous farm, healthy livestock, were all thriving and could have easily passed the rest of our lives right there.

But something else was deeply calling us and we couldn't turn away from it. The amazing part to me now, looking back, is to realize that we all felt the call. It was hard to leave home and yet we wanted to go more than we wanted to stay. There was a power to our family unit as we joined the others just before dawn and pushed off down the trail.

I will always remember my first home, the log walls, the blue calico curtains at the windows, the smoke circling out of the chimney, the sweet peas and violets along the gate.

Papa's brother Joshua and his family stayed behind to look after the farm and Grandma and Grandpa. They said we could come back if it didn't work out. I knew that we weren't coming back and that everything that I knew of life would never be the same from that moment on. The heaviness in my heart also had a sense of alive excitement right alongside of it.

Sometimes it all seems like a dream.

Love, Me

Thursday, July 15, 1852

So much has happened. Days pass into days and still we move along, miles away from my beloved parents.

We've passed over the summit of the Rocky Mountains. I expected a rugged, steep pass with precipices threatening us as we teetered along the edges. Never have I been so far from the truth.

South pass was a gentle and broad plain, the ascent so gradual that it was scarcely noticeable. I consider it a surprising gift and a blessing at this point of our journey, a sign of a possible ease ahead.

It's amazing to think that this is the dividing ridge which separates the waters flowing west into the Pacific Ocean from those which flow east into the Atlantic.

I've only read about high mountains. There's so much beautiful poetry written about mountains and the magic of them. I wrote a poem. I woke up last night and wrote it down.

For every man who walks the earth
the sun goes down
the sun goes down

For every man alive at birth

the sun goes down
the sun goes down

But life goes on in its special way
to bring each dawn and each new day
and with it someone to replace

the man the sundown takes away

I woke up with it ringing in my head and it wouldn't go away until I wrote it down. It just came out that way. I kind of like it. It came out as "man" but I know it's about a woman, too.

I don't think anyone can replace Mama or Papa. But Mama taught me to trust writing, just as it flows out, like water in a river. To let it flow where it wants, and it just might surprise you and take you somewhere full of wonder and delight.

So I did and that's what I wrote. I read it to Peter and he liked it. I don't know if I'll share it with anyone else, though. Aunt Sarah might think I was putting on airs with poetry.

Maybe I'll send it to Carrie, in my next letter. Someday I'll get letters back from her. But for now, it's healing to write to her. I can feel her reading them, crying softly about Mama and Papa.

Of course, Uncle Peter wrote too, a separate letter to the adults. But Carrie and Mama were real close. We all did our lessons with Mama. She made it so fun. We learned arithmetic from cooking, or from growing and measuring plants, or measuring for our clothes. We made up stories and plays, wrote them down and acted them out. We had spelling bees and learned the stars on clear, cold nights.

Somehow, I'm going to have to find a way to fill this big hole I feel in my heart. "Fill it with love," I can hear Mama say. I guess that is a good answer. Love for her and Papa, Peter and

Carrie and for life, for right now. Love that I am alive and can see the west and live there. I can feel us getting closer every day.

I am now sensing that real love and communication reach beyond the limits of time and space and even physical bodies and death.

Time to sleep. The moonlight makes everything glow and lights up the wagon. The night is alive with spirit.

Love, Me

Friday, July 16, 1852

My heart is breaking
could we stop for a moment?

wheels squeak, oxen mew, dogs scamper
trudge behind the wagon
pick up buffalo chips
keep my feet moving

my heart is breaking
could we stop for a moment?
a silent question
no one answers

the answer is no

Saturday, July 17, 1852

I've written two poems since Mama and Papa died. Mama loved poetry and we read some together. She wrote some poems too. I'm still so lost.

Nellie is a comfort—she sleeps with Peter and me at night. She howled when we buried Mama and Papa. When it was time to leave their graves, she whined and dug and wouldn't come. I had to pick her up and carry her and put her into the wagon, petting her and soothing her. She was feeling her own sorrow and seemed to have lost some of her spunk. But today she is trotting along behind the wagon again.

We made it over half way to the West before they died. Somehow, we will do this, Peter and I. People have been very kind to us. They know that "there but for fortune" goes one of their loved ones. Hans is still driving our wagon and teaching me how. In a few days, I will be able to do it alone. Papa would be proud of me for that.

Will I ever not feel the ache in my heart now? Some folks say we shouldn't have come west. And yet, I know that Mama and Papa are glad we did, even though they won't see the west. We will, and will grow up there and that's what they wanted.

Mama and Papa, I want to make you proud of me and glad that we went west, even though you are gone. Somehow, we will all know it was for the best, even though now I can only feel the deep emptiness of your loss. Tears can be cleansing, I hope, to wash away the pain.

Love, Me

Dear Nellie

Saturday, July 17, 1852

Dear Carrie,

It's been almost a week since I wrote last and we haven't passed anyone to take the letter, so I'll just keep going. It is a blessing to write to you and to sort out my feelings at the same time. I don't have anyone to talk to anymore with Mama gone. She would always listen, no matter how busy she was. We would talk while doing chores and that would make it fun.

Aunt Sarah just isn't like Mama. There's a different look in her eyes. It's not that she is a bad person, but she just doesn't like to talk. Maybe she thinks talking is bad.

I think talking airs out the soul and that it is not good to keep things all crammed up inside. It must get really stuffy for your insides and then there's no room for anything new.

Mama and Papa talked a lot, too. Seems like the more you can talk, the closer you can be. Aunt Sarah and Uncle Peter don't talk hardly and seem to operate in two separate spheres, which overlap out of necessity and cooperation.

It doesn't feel the same inside in my heart to be around them, not the same as it felt with Mama and Papa. From now on, and when I grow up, I want to feel like Mama and Papa which felt warm and good; the other way feels cold and hard.

I miss you and my home and Old Bessie. How is she? Burt thrives on all the challenges of riding and moving each day and then feasting on the long prairie grass.

All love, Katie

Sunday, July 18, 1852

I write to air out my soul. I write to use my mind and to record what I see and feel and know and don't know, and sometimes to discover what I do know.

The days pass quietly, within me, that is. There is so much happening on the outside, so much to see and do. The sorrow I feel is like a dark cloud which, little by little, eases away. Each day a tiny bit more blue sky and sun shine through. I know the sky is there behind the cloud, yet the darkness hangs around me still.

Mama always said that you have to feel the pain to feel the joy. I'm grateful for all the joy we had already.

Being with other families makes me see. We had more "love rich love," just for a shorter period. I will never lose their gift of love, which I carry in my heart. I carry you, Mama and Papa, in my heart. I want to write every day now. It calms my heart.

So many bright stars sparkle, like diamonds against the deep, blue velvet sky. The cool night air caresses my face and the candle makes shadows across the page. Peter sleeps near me. His quiet breathing soothes me. Nellie sleeps at his feet, dear sweet Nellie.

I feel very safe at this moment. I don't feel afraid any more–of the trip, of Indians, the west, any of it. If I tried to tell Aunt Sarah, she'd tell me I was being proud or give me a lecture about how I should watch out, etc. Somehow, I know deep down that the worst is over and we are going to be all right.

At this moment, looking at the dark sky and the shining stars, I am alone but I don't feel alone. I have discovered the "all one" in alone.

Love, Me

Monday, July 19, 1852

Oh the smell of the green grass and the feel of the clear, cool water on my face, on my body as I swam today. I found a little pool off of the Big Sandy River, where we nooned. Peter and I jumped in, clothes and all. We splashed and played like we hadn't since we left home.

Each time I remember about Mama and Papa, I feel a sharp pain in my heart. I still expect her to come around the bend. I even think I see her smiling and waving, calling to me. Then she's gone, like a mirage, fading into the air and nothingness, like the vapors that swirl over the rivers at night.

But for a few moments today, I forgot and let the water tickle me, soothe me, heal me. Since no one was around, I took off my dress and sat on the sand in my bloomers, and baked and soaked up the sun on my wet skin.

Aunt Sarah would faint if she knew I'd done such a thing. I could feel the sun seep down through my pores, filling me with her energy and light. Then I jumped back in to splash one more time.

They say we don't know when we'll find good water again, maybe for over forty-five miles. And after the Alkali of the Platte, I can see what they mean. This day and this time here in the river feel like a blessing, a small turning. Papa said not to worry about getting to the west, just to keep moving every day, giving our all, making time and working together.

Healing my heart must be a journey too. I have to trust that I will arrive at a place, one day, which could be called "healed." I know each day I inch forward, just as we roll along west.

Love, Me

Monday, July 19, 1852

Dear Carrie,

My heart seems bigger since I've come West. That may sound strange–it does even to me if I imagine you sitting in your kitchen reading this. But sitting here, right now, under the biggest sky I've ever seen or could ever have even imagined, it is true.

As Peter sleeps, I listen to his quiet breathing, so thankful he is still alive. I'd feel so alone without him and I know I help him, too. The stars shine bright. Remember how we used to watch the stars together and talk about God and all the wondrous subjects? I think about all those things a lot these days now that Mama and Papa are with Him.

I'm not as angry at God for taking them, though I have my moments of pure despair. I feel His presence and their presence and I even feel angels around me, watching and helping me. It's hard to explain in words, it's more of a sense.

But that's what I mean about my heart. Things seem to touch me more deeply now, like there's more heart to touch, deeper layers to feel. Even little things. People are kind to Peter and me, sharing, the tiniest things, and I feel it all in a new way.

I've made friends with a lady named Mrs. O'Malley. Today she gave Peter and me each a honey cake. Yum, what a treat!

Peter gave me an arrowhead he'd found. I cried when he gave it to me because I knew he was telling me that I was even more special to him than his arrowhead. I told him I'd share it with him because I knew it was his prize possession.

Tonight after supper we sang. What a treasure music is and how my heart glowed to sing the familiar songs. Everyone sang "Oh Suzanna," "Home Sweet Home" and "Old Folks at Home" with great gusto. I'm learning some new ones about the prairies. I'll write the words down for you when I learn them.

Aunt Sarah and Uncle Peter have been doing their best with us. They treat us well and yet they're so busy with their own children that I have a lot more freedom than I would have had, I guess.

Do you remember my French friend named Aurelie who is 12? Her mama has been very sweet to us and her papa calls her "ma petite rose"–my little rose. I'm learning some French songs and practicing more French.

I'm driving our wagon now and I must say I enjoy it. At first, I felt angry, knowing that I had to do it. But now I'm proud of being able to move the team, even down hills. Old Tom listens to me and when I say "Gee" he turns to the right and when I say "Haw" he turns to the left. Such a good and smart ox he is. Uncle Peter says I'm doing real well. My arms ached for the first few days but now they're used to it. Somedays I drive just by walking next to Tom, which is easier for the team.

Tomorrow we're fording the Big Sandy River and people are scared of quicksand. I don't know how we're going to do it. I'm praying extra hard tonight for angels to help us across. But somehow, I don't feel afraid. I think I buried my fear with Mama and Papa. I miss you.

Love from your cousin, Katie

Tuesday, July 20, 1852

We laid by an extra day to rest and feed the oxen and cut grass, putting it into burlap sacks to carry for when grass is scarce. We're about to hit a long dry stretch. We will rise and travel early tomorrow, rest during the mid-day and then travel long into the night. We all are turning in early to prepare.

Reading Mama's poetry book tonight, I came across an amazing poem called: "An Epitaph upon Husband and Wife, Which Died, and Were Buried Together," by Richard Crashaw. These are the words:

To these, whom death again did wed,
This grave's the second marriage-bed.

For though the hand of fate could force
'Twixt soul and body a divorce,
It could not sunder man and wife,
Because they both lived but one life.

Peace, good reader. Do not weep.
Peace, the lovers are asleep.
They, sweet turtles, folded lie
In the last knot love could tie.
And though they lie as they were dead,
Their pillow hard, and sheets of lead
(Pillow hard, and sheets not warm),
Love made the bed; they'll take no harm.
Let them sleep: let them sleep on,
Till this stormy night be gone,
Till the eternal morrow dawn
Then the curtains will be drawn
And they wake into a light
Whose day shall never die in night.

I guess it fit for them to die together like they did. Hard as it
is for me and Peter, I can't imagine one here without the other.
The biggest gift they gave me was their love. I know now that
love has a quality that is hard to describe. It can be so quiet that
you almost miss it but, like the moonlight, it lights up everything
and makes things clear, magical, special.

That poem seemed to be speaking right to me. I wonder if
Mama ever read it? I go to sleep with the thoughts of, "Peace,
good reader. Do not weep. Peace, the lovers are asleep." I can
sleep now. Peace is coming, slowly. I am reading the Bible
again.

Love, Me

Thursday, July 22, 1852

We passed yesterday across the longest stretch of dry and desolate country I could have ever imagined. We started at 4 am, rested mid-day, then alternated traveling and resting, pushing on until after midnight so that the teams could travel in the cool night air. We gave water and grass to the animals often and extra love and attention.

When we got close to the Green River, the teams could smell it, so we unyoked them and let them run ahead. They stood in the water, bawling, drinking, feasting, letting the water soak into their hides. I cried in joy for the end of their pain and loved to hear their happy sounds.

We'll rest here for a day to reward them for their hard work and difficult pull. Our train lost four head of cattle, and it broke my heart to see them suffer. I am learning to be strong in the face of life and death, but I still feel the pain of loss.

Love, Me

Friday, July 23, 1852

Some days writing is the only piece of myself that I know for sure is strong and true–the part that comes out on paper.

So much is changing. Every day a new place, new challenges and our ultimate destination, California, is new again.

And yet I am aware of some part of me that is unaffected by any of it. I remember sensing that in Mama and Papa, a quietness that was pure silence. They shared that and it overrode all their differences. It's hard to speak about. It's a knowing.

I'm very tired today. So many miles and so much dust. We're still waiting to ferry across the Green River. I'm thankful for the rest. Even with Papa gone, I still listen in at the men's meetings. Mr. Brown doesn't mind. Before we crossed the desert, he even asked me what I thought about resting or pushing on. I told him we should think of our animals first, that's what Papa would say, so we should rest extra. He agreed.

The aching in my heart quiets day by day. Peter is better, too. He has a new friend and they are hunting arrowheads all day, so he's tired at night and sleeps easier. I love him so.

Sweet Nellie is a comfort to us both and we're grateful to Rose for her milk and butter. Tom pulls hard still and Burt is always ready when I need to ride. These animals are my family too and I'll be grateful that they will be with us in our new life in the west.

Love, Me

Tom and the team

Saturday, July 24, 1852

Awoke dreaming of Mama and Papa. Then I remembered. I left their bodies back somewhere, a nowhere place of dust and rocks and sky. No trees. Mama would have liked a tree.

My tears were on her face the last time I saw her. Beautiful and peaceful. We covered over them. We said good-bye.

Spirits never die. I know that now. I feel it every night as I tuck Peter in and write by the candle in the wagon Papa formed with his strong hands. Mama and I gathered the feathers and sewed the covers for the pillows we sleep on. Mama is here in those pillows; I feel Papa in the wagon.

Some things are never born and never die. That's what I learned today under the western sky. Well, I actually didn't learn it because there are some things you can't learn, you just know. That's what I know in my heart is true.

No one to talk to about these things except Peter. I tell him about it and he listens. Their spirits are not dead. Just their bodies are gone away now. He still cries sometimes, but not as hard.

"Do you think Heaven can see the West?" he asked me tonight.

"Of course it can. Why the West must be a little piece of heaven from what I've heard," I answered.

I found a beautiful reading in the Bible tonight that helped me a lot. I prayed for guidance, opened it up and my eyes fell right upon it.

The Letter of Paul to the Philippians, Chapter 4
Finally, brethren, whatsoever things are true,
whatsoever things are honest, whatsoever things are just,
whatsoever things are pure, whatsoever things are lovely,
whatsoever things are of good report, if there be any virtue,
and if there be any praise, think on these things.

"Whatsoever things are true...think on these things..." If I close my eyes, I can feel Mama here with me and hear her truth.

"Everything changes, Katie. Every moment of life. Sometimes you can just feel it more than other times. But don't

be afraid of it. That's when you have to be strong and feel what never changes. Like your faith and your love. They are what you hold onto when the world seems to be moving a bit too fast."

Yes Mama, so many times I've thought of your words and your wisdom. Thank you for helping me to see the inside of life and not just the outside. Sleeping easier now, day-by-day, night-by-night.

Love, Me

Sunday, July 25, 1852
Dear Carrie,

I feel childhood slipping away, day by day, and womanhood creeping in. Sometimes I feel excited by the change, but I wish I had Mama to talk to. Everything in my world is changing. There seems to be nothing I can hold onto.

If Mama were here, she'd hold me real close, she'd listen and understand. Now I feel her in my heart.

If Papa saw that I was upset, he wouldn't say much, but he'd take me on a walk. We'd look at things in nature together. I remember walking with Papa through the fields. Overnight, it seemed, the rows of corn had grown taller than I was.

Papa said, "The wonder of it, Katie. Nature works silently, subtly. We don't even notice, then turn around and there it is— the corn so tall, the apple trees bursting with light pink blossoms, a peach plump with ripeness, a baby calf on the straw blinking at us. And all the time, we think nothing is happening. How easily we are fooled."

After that, I got to looking every day to see what magic nature had done. It became a game with Papa and me, to share what we'd noticed. I liked that game. It made me slow down, look, listen and feel the changes. Then change seemed more friendly. All the good that was going on all the time, that was change, too.

Now I look around and notice what I can sense that is new or different from the day before. It keeps me awake to the quiet side of life, the inside.

Oh, there's plenty happening on the outside, too. It's easy to get carried away by that. Miles to walk, rivers to cross, fuel to fetch, camp to make, washing to do, livestock to feed, care for and drive, food to prepare.

But my game has become to find the inside of experiences. Can I tell how the livestock are feeling? Sometimes I can. I just have to slow down, feel and listen to them, look at them. They might be sweating and overheated, or dry and parched. I can get them a sip of water or make sure at our next stop that they get good grass, plenty of water.

Or they might seem anxious by noises they hear, and if I listen, I can hear the noises, too—wolves or coyotes. Sometimes I can't figure out why they're anxious—maybe they sense a storm. But if I spend a few moments with them, they calm right down again.

They have become my friends, a soothing presence, a part of our home brought with us, a link from the past through the present to the future. Another life going west and hoping to make it alive.

I can almost imagine Papa there with me, sharing and laughing about all the things we noticed today. "Did you see the pretty new bird, Papa? It had a red breast and the sweetest song. It seemed to be singing just to me. I wonder if it had a nest and little babies? It wasn't afraid of me, Papa, and if we were staying on, it might have shown me its nest. I left it little crumbs of my biscuit and it swooped off with them. I didn't get to say good-bye to it. We had to leave and push on."

Missing Mama, Papa, my home and you.

Love, Katie

102

My little bird friend

Monday, July 26, 1852

We're in rough mountain country, but after the desert, I find the pine forests an oasis, and the streams clear and fine. We're on our way down to the Bear River.

Mrs. O'Malley is my friend and helps me fill the void in my heart. She always has a bit of biscuit for me and Peter or a smile, wink or a "how are ye today," (and she always really means it when she asks). She's traveling with her daughter and her daughter's husband and their two sons.

She's real good at cooking and washing and says you can make fine money in the mining camps just displaying female talents and hers are of the washing and cooking kind. But she's going West for more than that, I can tell. She's got joy in her eyes and the excitement of adventure on her face.

She'll do real well, too. I bet you could plant her anywhere and she'd do well. As it is, she does washing and cooking for lots of the other women just to help out and does it like it is nothing at all. She covers her plump form with a poplin dress of faded lavender flowers, and a white apron. Her graying hair is twisted up into a bun under her wide blue bonnet.

She always has the best smells coming from her kettle or her fire and you wonder why. She has the same ingredients as everyone else–flour and water and fat for the biscuits. But she stands over her fire, wiping her brow against the heat, smiling and singing softly to herself. That must be her secret ingredient. All her joy!

"What a glorious day," she'll say when it's lovely.

"Another day closer to the West," if it's dry or dusty, rainy or just generally bad.

Or just, "How's my Katie today?" to me. I can tell her, too, how I really am, and she listens.

Her good humor has made her admired and respected by all the other women and the men adore her because she's always sharing her tasty fixings. She's real handy at helping with mothers giving birth, too. We've had four so far on our journey. Aunt Sarah looks ready to have her baby any time now. I'm helping out more with the cooking. Mrs. O'Malley helps us lots. Got to sleep now.

Love, Me

Wednesday, July 28, 1852

Dear Carrie,

So much has happened. Oh joy of joys, Aunt Sarah gave birth to a baby girl yesterday. They named her Sharon. Oh Carrie, I'd forgotten how tiny and sweet babies are. Little pink hands and feet and puffy faces. Aunt Sarah was having a hard time and in a lot of pain. Mrs. O. (Mrs. O'Malley's nickname) bustled in and knew just what to do, her commanding presence putting everyone at ease.

She calmed everyone down, especially Uncle Peter. She sent him off to boil water. Then she gently pulled the baby out, got her all untangled from her cord and breathing while we all just gaped and blinked.

I cried to see baby Sharon, so fresh and new to life. Soon we were all crying and hugging, the baby and Sarah, Uncle Peter, me and Mrs. O. It was the happiest I've ever seen Aunt Sarah. She was hoping for a girl and what a beauty she is. You should see baby Sharon's chubby cheeks and curly brown hair.

We had to push on today. Sharon was born late yesterday. Aunt Sarah rested in the wagon today and the baby slept a lot. I imagine that the wagon's rocking is just like a cradle for her. I hold her to help out and I love to rock her gently and feel her sleep against my chest. She looks right at me and though they say tiny babies can't see, I know she sees me and I smile back at her with all the love in my heart.

I talk to her too and tell her how glad we are that she's here and that she needs to eat a lot and stay really healthy because we're going west and it's kinda hard. But once we get to California, she'll have a nice home with a cozy fireplace.

The other little baby born last week, a boy, died and so did his Mama. The papa was so broken up about it that he nearly didn't go on. But his brother took him in and carried him along for a few days. Uncle Peter helped out too.

Someone else had to drive his wagon. He just stared. After a few days, he was able to drive the wagon again and I notice now he's helping with the chores as before. But he doesn't say much. We feel his sorrow and I am extra thankful for baby Sharon.

Life can slip away so fast, just like the shooting stars that zip across the sky and are gone. Some stars move faster and some are slower and longer. I hope, Carrie, that my life can shine brightly and when I die, that my spirit can fly across the heavens in a giant burst of bright light, raining silver dust behind me.

As I write, my little cousin sleeps gently by my side. She's as tiny as a peanut, but sturdy and strong. She'll make it, I know she will and I'm glad.

Tonight when I say my prayers and thank-yous to life, I'll be sure to say thank you for her first. I send the joy in my heart to you across the miles and I wish you many blessings.

Love from your cousin, Katie

Thursday, July 29, 1852

Today I felt so angry, furious. Riding was all I could think to do. I rode ahead of the train on Burt. He let me ride and ride. He loved it too, I could tell. It helped me some, but I still feel upset.

Is there such a thing as just angry and not really at anyone? Mama used to say it was a good sign to be angry after you've been blue, that it meant you were coming out of it.

Maybe, but it's uncomfortable, too. I feel like I'm getting hard inside and I don't like that. It comes partly from not having Mama and Papa to talk to, no one to trust. Mrs. O'Malley is always there, but it's hard to go up to her, in the middle of things and I usually burst into tears, even if I'm angry. Guess I'll go and talk to her. Can't feel any worse from it.

Love, Me

PS I looked up furious in the dictionary and the root of it is "fury." That makes sense. I felt fury.

Thursday, July 29, 1852

Dear Carrie,

Feeling a little better tonight. Just talked to Mrs. O'Malley. She helped me a lot. I was so angry, just at the world, I guess, because life isn't the way I thought it would be. Mrs. O'Malley always knows wise words to say to me. Mostly she just listens. Seems that's what most people want and need anyway, listening.

She even says, "The good Lord gave us two ears and one mouth, but do you think people listen more than they talk? No." But she does and my heart feels some lighter, but there's still darkness inside.

Guess when you read these letters, you're sure glad you're not here with us. Yet in spite of all the pain we've been through, every day we move along and it is an amazing feeling, being like gypsies, with our wagons, headed west.

Don't know as I'll ever have an adventure quite like this one and there is a part of me that knows that and is separate from all the sorrow and anger that pours out of my heart. We witness courage every day and the human spirit which will survive, no matter how challenging the circumstances.

People help each other a lot. Not just within families, but among the train members and even with other trains, there's a give and take. There's a preacher who walks, no wagon at all, and Mrs. O'Malley cooks for him.

A butterfly just landed on my shoulder as I sit in the mid-day sun. Butterflies must not be angry or blue, they're too light for that. What do you think, Carrie? Missing you from the West.
Love, Katie

Friday, July 30, 1852

Summer is peaking now. Clear bright days dawning, soft warm nights that embrace me and lull me to sleep.

We're camped at Ham's Fork of the Bear River in a grove of fir and aspen trees. I look out over the valley of the Bear River as the moon rises over the ridges. A perfect moment except for the persistent mosquitoes that interrupt my writing as I hit at them with my hand.

Another baby born today. We stopped early this afternoon and will begin again tomorrow. Everyone washed and tidied up. I had to clean out our wagon and do the washing for Peter and me. Mrs. O'Malley helps me a lot. Aunt Sarah can't right now, she needs my help.

I remember Sharon's birth three days ago and smile. She didn't cry and she looked right into my eyes. She seemed calm, awake. Watching her birth filled me with wonderment. How can we possibly create another life from inside our bodies? Time to sleep.

Love, Me

Saturday, July 31, 1852

The wagon rocks Baby Sharon like Grandma's old cradle, and she sleeps as we roll along. I'm glad, because Aunt Sharon couldn't bring her cradle with her on this trip and she mourned for it. Now she smiles that the wagon doubles as a cradle. Sometimes Aunt Sarah wears Sharon in a sling, which Mrs. O'Malley made for her.

Sharon seems content to be a part of things. There's no time for resting after births, so only the strongest survive. Papa used to say that about animals and in nature, but I never thought of it for people before. Out here, on this trail, it is very clear that nature reigns.

People just have to go on after a loss, but it hurts. The young Papa who lost his wife and son still struggles. Oh how I understand. He was thinking of turning back but Uncle Peter talked to him and encouraged him to go on. The newness of the journey may help him to recover faster.

Aunt Sarah needs me to help with Sharon. New life is something to rejoice over.

Love, Me

Baby Sharon

Sunday, August 1, 1852

Camped along the Bear River and laying over for the Sabbath. The cattle wade in wild oats up to their ears and I'm so glad. They deserve a feast. They gain strength for the last part of our journey. Mrs. O'Malley made corn candy and cookies today. Yum. I feel quieter and calmer every day, and stronger, too.

The memory of Mama and Papa soothes me and guides me to live the destiny we all had written in us.

From Mama, I learned the beauty of words, books, fine laces and dishes, old treasures she had from her Grandmama that were really special, like they don't make any more. We had to leave most all of that behind. But the words we brought in our minds and in our hearts and can draw upon anytime we want to or need to.

We used to make up stories, to create with words because we only have a few books along. Books are my dolls, stories my friends, words my companions. We brought a book of poems, the Bible and each brought our own favorite storybook, one we could read over and over. I've already read these and all the other books in the whole wagon train, at least three times.

Mama talked about finding new meaning in the words, even if you've read them before. "You never read it from where you are today," she said. "You can learn something entirely new this time." She was right. I can hear her speaking to me and feel her gentle presence beside me as I read and write.

Mama said that your mind can be like rich soil where you can plant a seed and then nurture it and it will grow into a beautiful flower which can give you so much pleasure. But like growing a real flower, you have to take care of it, be patient, let it grow at its own pace and give it room and space. I will always remember that.

Papa said the same things about nature. Pay attention, listen, feel the flowers bloom, sense the animals and what they need and give them that. I can see now that whether it is words or nature, it is all the same. Find the depth and grace in the simple things and then find them again, in a new moment and it will be different and ever so shining and good.

What I realize now is that Mama and Papa taught me the same lessons, only from different points of view.

Time to sleep. Tears and prayers. My heart is healing.

Love, Me

Monday, August 2, 1852

Dear Carrie,

Life goes along pretty smoothly these days. We're in a real routine. Up each day at dawn, gather the animals, help Aunt Sarah with the cooking, pack up and leave. The little ones sleep in the wagon until later, then I help out with them, if needed.

When I'm not driving the wagon and oxen, (my friend Tom helps me by taking turns) I walk behind and keep the livestock from straying off. I like the walking. I'd much rather walk than sit, though driving the wagon is fun.

I'm watching Peter sleep. He looks so much like Mama with his dark hair. How sweet and good he is. He trusts me absolutely and his little heart is mending slowly.

Mama told me to stay in my heart. I'm beginning to understand what she meant. It seems like there are different types of people. Just like people look different on the outside because of where they come from, people must look different on the inside too, because they sure act that way.

It seems like some think in their heads and others in their hearts. Mama and Papa and Peter and I, we feel life, from our hearts. Grandmama, she thinks life, from her head. I'm so glad I'm not like that. It seems stale, dry, empty, with no depth or substance to it.

For example, Grandmama was dead set against us coming west. Now she will just say that she was right, with Mama and Papa gone. It's a good thing she can't find us or she'd order us home to her. I wouldn't be happy about that at all.

Grandmama couldn't feel the west in her heart like we could. How it pulled us and is still pulling us and for all the pain and loss, it feels so good to be pulled. Now this is not something that you can explain to a head person. Even some of the people on our train are coming west for thinking reasons. Lots of land, gold, opportunity, those are all good and rational reasons to come. But there's more and I don't even know if I can put it into words.

I guess that's what Mama meant when she said that words would keep me company. It's like I'm chasing them around trying to catch the ones to say what is in my heart. Sometimes I catch them and sometimes they get away, but it is always a fun game.

Sometimes I see people who are head people slip and open up and for a moment, they are heart people. It seems like they must really be heart people masquerading as thinking people—like they think it is better to not feel or something. I don't ever want to lose feeling about life. It's like a magic secret. Mama and Papa never lost it, so Peter and I won't either. It's up to me to make sure we don't.

There's a man named Pater who still has the accent from his country in Europe. He's in his early twenties and he smiles at me. He told me he has a little sister back home and misses her very much. He is nice. He gave me some pink wild roses. But mainly he just smiles. His English is not very strong yet and Aurelie's Papa can speak to him, so he spends a lot of time with them.

Time to sleep again. Dawn comes early, but I'm always glad for a new day, a little closer to the west and a little lighter in my heart. Missing you from farther and farther west.

Tuesday, August 3, 1852

A man on the train whips his son Noah, just like he whips his animals. He joined up with us after we lost over half our train to cholera.

I can see the pain in Noah's eyes. His Papa is killing off Noah's spirit, one whipping at a time, but he's too righteous to notice. The Papa becomes an angry whipping machine and Noah retreats to a place way inside his soul.

Uncle Peter finally spoke to the Papa. It wasn't easy because the man is righteous toward everyone, not just Noah. What Uncle Peter said was very wise, I felt.

He told Mr. F. that his views on child rearing were his own to choose. But while we were all together here as one family, working toward our common survival, we had to take the mean belief into account. Uncle Peter had spoken to each family and they all agreed that Noah's beatings were too extreme. Mr. F.

had a choice: Lay off the whippings, or move on to another train. The pastor is also talking to him.

It has been two weeks now and Noah appears to be a person set free. He's sixteen and he told me that when he gets to California, he's leaving. I understand. I would too. Maybe he can get himself back, dig himself out from under all that anger which has been dumped on him for so long. I don't know. He acts like a wounded soldier with glimpses of life before pain and distant memories of peace.

Prayers of thanksgiving for my loving family and the freedom in my soul. All Love, Me

Wednesday, August 4, 1852

Those of us who are left know that we have to be strong and keep going for all the loved ones we've buried along the way. We can't give up no matter how hard it becomes. They push us over the mountains, they're with us through the rushing rivers, and over the long and dry deserts. Last night I could feel their presence as the moon rose over the long and lonesome trail and the coyotes and wolves howled their songs to the skies.

The sunsets are the prettiest I've ever seen and the contrast between the huge sky and the never-ending land is a wondrous sight to my eyes and senses. I'm glad when I get to walk, to feel the earth under my feet. Aunt Sarah says that's the wonder of youth–walking and not tiring. Besides, then I can walk with the livestock and they are really good company. Old Tom is still my favorite of the oxen. He's holding up real well under the trip. Papa knew he would.

Even though he is the oldest of our team, he is strong and determined. He pulls slow and steady and keeps on going. I guess that's what's required on this trip. I give him pats and talk into his ear sometimes. I can almost imagine him smiling at me. Sometimes he snorts. At night, I give him some extra grass and always make sure he has water and a good place to sleep.

Peter is doing better. A new family joined our train and he has a new friend and they are inseparable.

I miss the farm and growing things. Aurelie's mother is teaching us to gather herbs and plants that help when you're sick or needing something from nature. She's real good at that and everyone has come to rely on her when anybody takes sick. Back on the farm, Papa and I used to love to work together and wonder at how things grew.

That brings up the green thumb. Grandpa, Papa's pa had the green thumb. Papa had it and told me I did too. He smiled about that. He said folks acted like it was some kind of luck with plants, but he knew better. He said it was an interest in plants, liking them, caring for them, treating them with respect for the fact that they are alive, just like we are. It's looking them over and seeing what they need and giving them that.

Papa used to chuckle about the green thumb as we tended the little seedlings. I remember when I was about three, he taught me how to put them into the ground. "We tuck them in, see, like I do for you when we say goodnight. Just pat real gentle around them." I even would say, "nighty night little plants," and Papa would chuckle some more.

He even gave me my own little garden, which I would tend, watering, weeding, loosening up the soil around the plants, talking to them, caring for them. I'd watch Papa to make sure I wasn't forgetting anything.

"You've got to feel the soil, Katie, to see if it is right for planting and then to know if it is too dry or wet. When it is just right, it feels light, loose." Slowly, tenderly, Papa passed on his green thumb to me.

I remember that Grandmama used to frown when she would see the dirt under my fingernails. I tried to get it out, but sometimes it just wouldn't budge. She'd scold Mama and say that I was becoming a wild thing.

Mama would shake her head and smile. "It's life on a farm and a joy in nature. If that's wild, then that is a good wild." Grandmama would just frown some more and sniff. But that was just her way. She was old and I guess the older you get the harder it is to change.

I don't ever want to get too old to change. Maybe if I start right now always welcoming change, by the time I'm as old as Grandmama, I won't think of it as bad. I hope so.

I asked Aurelie's mom if she had the green thumb, but she had never heard of it. I guess in France, they don't have it or else they call it something else.

My heart is healing, the west is calling, time to sleep.

Love, Me

Thursday, August 5, 1852

Enjoying the peace and quiet today. We stopped to noon, to rest the animals, make repairs, wash up clothes and us. There's excellent water and grass. Everyone is very happy about that. Lots of game, too. We'll have a stew tonight. Yum. Which reminds me, I'm hungry a lot of the time. Aunt Sarah says I'm growing like a prairie weed. I've outgrown my two dresses.

Mrs. O'Malley is helping me to sew in pieces along the sides and hem. Aunt Sarah loaned me a dress till we've fixed mine. Uncle Peter says I've grown a good six inches. Is that possible?

I'd be almost as tall as Mama and Papa now. I feel a bit gangly and awkward with all this new height. I'm not quite used to it.

But my longer legs are great for riding Burt. It's much easier to swing over him now or jump off. Walking along by the wagon, I stride ahead and leave Peter in the dust. He has to run along to keep up, just like I used to do with Papa.

With Mama and Papa gone, I'm responsible for Peter and me. I unload our bedding, set up the tent, if we use it, unyoke the oxen from the wagon. Peter helps me a lot, we work as a team. He's real good with the animals. I don't have to cook for us, but I do help Aunt Sarah or Mrs. O'Malley.

Some washing days, I have to do a lot of ours, but I can always ask for help. My main job is to watch out for Peter and help him through this time and to drive our wagon when Tom doesn't do it. I also help with baby Sharon a lot, but I love that. Peter is getting stronger every day, though he still hurts sometimes, but then so do I. We can help each other with that.

Love, Me

Thursday, August 5, 1852

Dear Carrie,

Rose, the milk cow, trudges steadily along. Every morning I milk her and put part of her cream into the covered bucket. Remember how I told you how the wagon rocking churns the butter? So we have butter by evening and fresh buttermilk. Yum.

Tonight Peter caught some fish in the stream and Mrs. O'Malley fried them right up for us. Aunt Sarah doesn't mind her helping us out. Aunt Sarah has her hands full with her three little ones. I take baby Sharon whenever I can, mostly when I'm walking.

116

If Sharon is fretting, she quiets right down and when I pick her up, she smiles at me. She's snug in the fabric sling we made for her. She looks out, wide-eyed. I wonder how being born in the wild will affect her life? Will she be even more drawn to what is wild in her and in life? I look forward to watching her grow and meeting over and over the beautiful flower she will become.

She's my special little cousin. Maybe she'll call me Katie, like Elizabeth did. I would like that. Oh Carrie, I so look forward to your letters again someday. I've memorized your five and so wish I had more.

Everything flows west from here except my letters to you! Hugs and kisses from west of the Rockies.
Love, Katie

Saturday, August 7, 1852

I saw an eagle today, a real gift. There are lots of eagles, but this one sat for a while and I got to watch it. I found comfort in the thought that this eagle belongs to the same family as my eagles back home.

I made up a story tonight for Peter, about the baby eagle that was afraid to jump out of the nest. But finally she did and soared and swooped and flew with her Mama. He loved it until we got to the Mama part. I should have thought of that. I held him close and we sat for a while.

"I know," was finally all I said. "It will be better over time, Peter. Mama said to feel the pain. That's all we can do. It's a part of life, too."

Helping Peter has helped me more than I could have ever known. I've had to dig down deep into my own wisdom and draw it out for him. Some things I tell him, I didn't even know I knew till there they are coming out of my mouth. There's a discovery in sharing with another. I'm learning a lot about life.

117

Mama used to say a life was like a tapestry, rich in colors, textures and designs. That it couldn't just be say, blue. Or that if it was, it would not be as powerful.

I remember the day we talked about that. She told me about my birth.

"Oh Katie, that would have been the brightest of colors–orange and yellow and red for the last of the fall leaves as they fell softly outside the window on that first day of November.

Then white and blue black for the moon shining through the trees against the dark night sky. Then purple and red for the pain of your birthing. Papa sat with me, held my hand, stroked my hair, all through. Grandma helped with your birth.

Then bright yellow for the pure joy I felt looking into your eyes, holding you close, hearing you suck on your fingers as you surveyed the room. You didn't even cry. You seemed to be saying, "Hello Mama. I'm glad I'm here. We have a lot to learn and to share."

"See Katie, that's how you colored my life. There was so much more than pain there. The pain was just a piece of it."

Yes, Mama, I'm beginning to see. I still miss you so. Tears of love, now, not as much sorrow.

Love, Me

Sunday, August 8, 1852

I saw the eagle again today. He sat quiet, still. I sat too. It was nooning time, the time of the day when there's a moment to catch a breath.

I sat by the creek, a little away from camp, as I like to do, to jot down thoughts or sketch a scene. He soared above me, circled, then perched atop a dead pine, just ahead of me, down the slope toward the river. We looked at each other.

I feel it is a gift to be in an eagle's gaze, maybe like having an audience with the president or a king. He stared at me off and on, then gazed at the splendor about him below. We shared the view. A green velvet hillside, sloping down to the river. The silver blue water glistening in the bright sun.

I played a game papa and I used to play, when we would encounter a bird or animal. We'd be real quiet and listen for their words. So I listened for the eagle's words.

"This is good," he said. "There is beauty here."

I agreed and waited.

He turned to look at our wagons, lined up in disarray. I sensed more words coming.

"Do not destroy the beauty you see here."

I felt his words, and a wave of shame flooded my face, tingling my scalp. I thought of all the debris I'd seen along the trail–wagon pieces, forlorn rockers, warped from rain, a mercantile of china, utensils, clothes. They were once such prized possessions that they couldn't be left behind. Now they were left along the wayside, useless to all, where lighter loads meant survival, heavy weight, certain death.

I sensed more words. "Only man can destroy this beauty." I knew what he meant.

He looked at me again. I heard, "You must learn from this day." He paused, then swooped down over me and soared up above the grove of trees on the ridge. I spotted him again that afternoon, three more times. Each time, I heard his words, echoing off the trees, whispered by the wind. "You must learn from this day."

I search for the meaning of his words and ask myself, "what did I learn from this day?"

I learned again the value of listening, of being quiet so that I could hear his words. I learned the value of time, of taking time for Peter, to listen to him and comfort him. Of taking time to write, and to share with Mrs. O'Malley, and to care for baby Sharon.

The eagle has time. He's not rushed or frightened. He moves with wisdom, yet power, waiting, striking fast when he has to.

What I learned from this day, Mr. Eagle, is that I must learn from each day or I have turned my back on a precious gift.

I sense his words. "Very good." I wrap myself in the glow of his approval as I feel the soft night inviting me to sleep. Lots of shooting stars!

Love, Me

The eagle

Monday, August 9, 1852

Just as many have had to leave possessions behind, cluttering along the trail, there are ideas we've let go of too, invisible though they may be. I feel them hovering about with the trunks, china, goblets and kettles, alongside the trail.

Grandmama used to scold me for sitting on the floor, unladylike it was, she scoffed. Well Grandmama, we don't even have a floor now and we sit wherever we can, unladylike or no. And then there's the topic of women needing privacy for nature's calls, something not even discussed. Well, there is no privacy here, and the spaces with no trees make life a real challenge.

The women group together, holding out skirts to create a barrier, nothing else to do about it. At the beginning, we could slip behind a tree or bush. But later there were no trees or bushes to be had. So we've had to help each other out as best as we can.

Oh Grandmama would frown and purse up her lips in horror if she knew what "wild things" we've become.

I feel compassion for Grandmama. I feel her pain of losing Mama and her pain sits atop of her not understanding why and the two will keep each other alive and never be settled. At least I know in my heart why we are here and my pain has a peaceful place to settle down and calm.

Someday I will see Grandmama again and I hope my strength will be such that I can help her and not judge her. She loved Mama and us in her way. I can see that now. Sending her peace and love from here.

Love, Me

Tuesday, August 10, 1852

We keep moving steadily on. We're on our way to Fort Hall. I'm a little better every day. I feel Mama and Papa here with us, but just not in physical form.

Someday I will have a whole room full of books with Mama's in a place of honor. Meanwhile, I'm reading them over and over and learning every single word and all its meanings from the dictionary. Between that and teaching Peter his lessons, our evenings pass quietly. It's what Mama would want me to do and I feel a real peace doing it.

I can almost imagine that nothing has changed and yet now it is me who must be strong and carry on. Mama showed me so well. It's easy to be loving and patient with Peter. It is our special time.

Mama brought the Bible, a dictionary and a special book of poems. She said that poetry packed the most meaning into the fewest words. I guess she is right. She also said that you can read a poem every day and get a new meaning out of it each time, like it was brand new.

The dictionary would help us to learn and we could make up our own stories from learning new words. We could play games with words and try to guess what they mean. We did that and it was fun. Learning new words helps me to find new ways to express my feelings and that feels good.

Mama taught me to look at the roots of words. Lots of the roots are Latin or Greek or French. It becomes a game to discover the origin of the word.

I learned today that the word comfort comes from the Latin root "to strengthen." I feel that my comforting Peter has allowed me to feel my strength and to share it with him and I'm thankful for that. We've both been comforted, we've both gained strength.

I also am learning that being strong does not mean to not feel. I still cry when I need to and so does Peter. I know that there is a special strength and comfort in feeling what is true. I feel the sorrow, but I also feel the deep joy and wonder of going to a new place beyond where others have gone and where a new life awaits us all.

I wonder at moving on each day–new places, sights and smells. The older folks worry a lot, but I wake in amazement each morning to remember we're headed west, exploring, discovering. I feel myself being part child, part woman now. The child in me runs and plays with Peter and it is fun. The woman part feels to the depths of my soul the gift it is to begin to live a new life in a place that is free and open.

Life does go on. That is for sure. We're getting closer every day.

Love, Me

Tuesday, August 10, 1852

Dear Carrie,

Remember how we used to talk about angels? Well, I've been thinking a lot about them lately. Mama and I used to talk about them, too. Maybe it's all the space out here and so few people, but I seem to be sensing them more. I realize that angels are not just invisible fairy-like spirits with wings. They can also be real people who come along in your life and help you, give you gifts.

Mrs. O'Malley is an angel for sure. She's the kind you get to keep for a while. Well, for me, a few months on this trip, and maybe longer. But sometimes angels are here and gone in a flash.

Like yesterday. We were going along as usual. We rose early, traveled as best we could and were stopped for our mid-day rest. The teams were eating and everyone was peaceful. Along came a man on a beautiful black horse. I suspected that he was an angel right off because he was riding alone and because his horse was so special. (I think angels travel alone so as to appear and disappear easily.)

Well, he rode in real fast and stopped in a cloud of dust right next to the wagon master. He was a real smart looking fellow with a fine gray hat pulled down to shade his face. I went over to see the horse and pet her and to listen while he and Mr. Brown conversed.

The horse confirmed that he was an angel. She told me that he rode like the wind–light and easy on her back, no weight really, and blended in with her as he rode. She looked at me and flicked her ears up when she said that, then stomped her right foot for emphasis.

"Tough going up ahead," the angel said.

"That so," said Mr. Brown, scratching his head on the side as he looked up, shading the sun with his dusty, brown felt hat.

"Yeah, not much grass left on the trail, or water. But I just came over another way and I think you can get through with your wagons. There's good grass and a clear spring and you could make it by dusk. Look for the dead oak, go right there. You'll see the deer and Indian trail and just keep on it. There's one narrow spot, but you should just make it. Best of luck to ya!"

And with that he rode off, as fast as he rode in. He disappeared around a corner and I bet that right after he was out of sight, he was gone. I wish I could have peeked. Just before he left he turned and I saw his face. He was tanned from the sun and his brown hair was damp from the heat.

His blue-green eyes looked at me for a moment and that's when I knew he was an angel. There was an emptiness in those eyes and yet they were as full as the sky. He looked right into my soul in one instant. I looked right back. "Thank you," I said, without a sound. He tipped his hat and was off.

We took his course and went right at the dead oak tree, found the one narrow spot, eased through and got to the spring just before dusk. There was an air of celebration as we settled near the clean, fresh water. The teams ate their full and it was so lovely, shady, clean and rich that Mr. Brown decided that we should lay over one day to wash, cook and rest.

Thank you, Mr. Angel, wherever you are. And thank you, Carrie, for being an angel in my life. You will always be my oldest and dearest friend. Someday our children can be friends. Now that's a thought.

"For he shall give his angels charge over thee, to keep thee in all thy ways..." Psalms 91:11

Love and Hugs, Your cousin, Katie

Fiddle

Wednesday, August 11, 1852

Because we were laying over, we got to have fiddling, dancing and singing. Sometimes we have music, on the spur of the moment. But tonight, with the Bear River right here, we got to have a bath and be clean. Oh yes. I love that.

The dancing is so fun. I love to dance and I make Peter dance with me. He's a little wild sometimes and then he runs off too, but he does it for me and I think he even enjoys it a little, though he'd never admit it.

Papa used to dance with me and I know all the steps. Sometimes when I'm dancing, I feel like I am flying. The music and the movement and the fresh evening air on my face fill me with joy. I get dizzy with the fun and the celebration of it.

Everyone laughs and smiles when there is fiddling. That's good because there isn't one person on this train who hasn't lost someone or something or had to dig down deep into their hearts for strength to keep going.

Somehow, I feel that the worst of our troubles have passed. Nicely tired and clean as I fall asleep.

Love, Me

Thursday, August 12, 1852

"The morning stars sang together" The Book of Job

A song of silent strings
soothing my aching heart

airing out my soul in the
spaces between the stars

Another short poem. Wanting to try to express all the feelings that are bursting in me.

I feel the insignificance of my tiny human life and yet all at the same moment, I know I matter as a part of this huge whole. I'm a twinkling star too.

It matters that I am watching from where I am.

Excited to be alive today!

Love, Me

Friday, August 13, 1852

We're in hilly country now, pretty easy going. We passed Soda Springs, with one spring named Beer Springs. Uncle Peter says it doesn't taste at all like beer, but tastes mostly of sulfur. Oh the smell! Peter and I held our noses, but I liked the one called Steamboat Springs because it made a noise somewhat like a steamboat. We still plugged our noses, though and I was glad to move on.

Peter caught fresh trout and he and I found some strawberries, which we shared with Uncle Peter, Aunt Sarah and the boys. Mrs. O. gave us biscuits, so we had strawberry short cake topped with some of Rose's cream. Oh such a treat. Peter was ecstatic.

I watch his thin body while he sleeps. At this moment he so resembles Grandpa, the same wide forehead, huge hands and feet, like a puppy. Papa had the same strong hands. I look at Peter and see the link of time–his face and hands, Papa's and Grandpa's.

I look at my hands as I write these words. I don't have the same big hands.   Mine are thin, with long fingers–good for milking though and strong anyway. I guess my hands are like Peter's body, strong and thin. That thought made me laugh out loud and Peter started in his sleep. Nellie sleeps at his feet. Tired and growing.

Love, Me

Friday, August 13, 1852

Dear Carrie,

When I see the stars at night, I can feel my heart, as big as the sky and it swells with love and life. I see many shooting stars and they always feel like blessings, so I wish on them.

I wish for Peter to be happy and strong and to grow up to be a fine man. He will and I can help.

I wish for the West to be a place filled with goodness, energy and life. I feel it is.

I wish for freedom, for myself, to live my life in my own way, to find my life inside of myself and then in the West. I feel like a flower that will bloom and be strong, but right now is getting her roots established so she can stand up straight and tall.

Mama used to say that we are all special, that there has never been anyone like us before and that there never will be in the future. Don't you think that's an amazing thought? I do. But a wonderful one too. Not in a prideful way like—"Look at me, I'm special," but rather, "look at everyone, we're all special."

This thought has been accompanying me along the way as I walk and herd the cattle or drive the wagon. What is unique and special about everyone and everything? As I'm talking to some of the people on the train, I notice them really carefully. How are they special?

Missing you and your specialness to me.

All Love, Katie

Saturday, August 14, 1852

Taking some comfort in the Bible. Mrs. O'Malley suggested I read the Psalms. I found a few passages that helped me.

"Weeping may endure for a night, but joy cometh in the morning" Psalms 30:5:

That is how I feel. Nights are hard, mornings better, the freshness of the new day giving me hope, the adventure ahead filling me with energy and enthusiasm.

Mrs. O'Malley knitted me a pouch to carry my writing book in. That way I can jot things down during the day as I think of them, or stop and sketch a scene that I want to remember for all time. She didn't have much schooling, so she enjoys the fact that I can write about how I feel and what I see.

Sometimes I read to her what I've written, in the evenings, while she's sewing or mending. I read her the poems from Mama's book, too. She can read the Bible, though, real well. She says she knows a bit of it by heart, especially the Psalms.

Mrs. O'Malley comforts me with her love and I am grateful.

Love, Me

Sunday, August 15, 1852

We had a short church service. Preacher Smith read from the Bible while folks worked on repairing and simple tasks.

Everyone listens attentively, but we have to use every minute to reach our goal.

For the hymns at the end, we all gather together in a circle. I love the singing and always stand next to Mrs. O'Malley. She sings loud and strong and seems to feel the music. She cried during some of the songs and so I asked her why.

"Oh, it's just heart feeling tears. When your heart is just going to burst with love."

"Is it alright that I don't cry when I sing?"

"Oh yes. You feel joy. That is good. Mine is joy, too. A different flavor, but joy all the same."

I do feel joy again. It's like the fresh air of the west. It blows through my heart and soul and fills me with energy and love.

Baby Sharon is a love. Peter grows like a weed. No one would recognize him. I guess I've grown, too, inside and out.

"Thine eyes did see my substance... and in thy book all my members were written...when as yet there was none of them." Psalms 139:16

I've been thinking about how I have a world inside me and then there's the world outside. We're all looking at the same outside world, but how we see it must be colored by how we think and feel—our inside world.

Oh how I miss mama right now. I could talk to her about that. She would tell me that no one else has my inside world or my particular view of the outside world, so writing about it counts. Yes, mama, thank you.

I'm also noticing how when I write or sit quietly, I feel peaceful and hear my own answers. Could that be my soul talking to me?

Peaceful and tired,

Love, Me

Monday, August 16, 1852

We're a close group now because we are of a like mind. There's no bickering like there used to be or arguing among the men. Mr. Brown has gained the respect of all of us and we work together for our common driving desire–to be in California before the fall cold settles into the mountains. He says that's why we do so well and make such good time.

Mr. Brown figures that we average fifteen miles on good days. Some days get lost in the crossing of rivers or in sand that slows us to a near halt, but mostly we move along. The steadiness and the changing terrain give us all hope and encouragement. Almost to Fort Hall.

Love, Me

Tuesday, August 17, 1852

We arrived at Fort Hall and are laying by for a few days. It's good to let the stock have a rest to gorge on the plentiful grass.

Aunt Sarah scolded me for going to the fort alone. I just had to see it and took Burt out when all was quiet, saying I was just going for a ride. I liked the adventure of going by myself. It was worth the upbraiding.

The Fort didn't have many supplies and what they had were expensive. Back in Independence, flour sold for four dollars a barrel, but here they were charging one dollar for a pint!

But I traded some of Rose's milk to a fur trader and he agreed to carry my letters east to Carrie. When Uncle Peter found me at the Fort, he let me stay to trade with him. He got some coffee, but paid a dollar for a pint.

The Snake Indians inhabit this territory and seem friendly. Mrs. O'Malley traded one of her pies for some deer meat and made a stew with an onion and some potatoes she had saved. She shared the stew with us.

I gave her the last of our dried apples for the pies. We feasted on the stew and the pie, with cream from dear Rose. I found some mint and we made mint tea. It feels like not only the animals need to rest up and fatten up for the rest of the journey. Guess we do too.

The mint tea reminded me of Mama and I felt the ache of missing her. But then I got to play with Aurelie some and learn some new French words. Thé à la menthe. That's mint tea in French. Mama would be proud.

Love, Me

Fresh mint, so sweet

Wednesday, August 18, 1852

The sky is fairly popping with stars. I can't sleep yet. Everything is quiet around me. I can hear the howling of a wolf echoing along the river canyon. The moon is dark and there are no shadows tonight. How I love to peek out into the night from our cozy wagon. Evenings are cooling off now as the fall approaches. Nellie lifts up her head and pricks her ears at the wolves.

Today I saw a mama quail and her babies. I was walking a little behind and I startled them as I turned a corner. She ran off screeching to the left and her babies ran to the right. I stood totally still. As I waited, I realized that she ran left and screeched to distract me from her babies. She would have sacrificed herself for them.

As I listened, she called out to them and ran across to find them again. She was a fine mother. I don't think I'll ever be able to eat quail again. I'd rather dine on dry biscuits and beans than to disturb the beauty I witnessed today.

Later, I had a good talk with Mrs. O'Malley. She hums as she washes and cooks. Her blue eyes smile from her heart, as she looks right into mine. She gives me the best hugs and tells me how well I'm doing and how grown up I'm becoming.

"A heart is not real till it's broken a wee bit, you know."

"Really?" I asked.

"Of course. Then it can grow bigger and just keep on growin'. A huge heart has no boundaries from one to the next. Now that is happiness."

"Hmm. I'll have to think on that one," I said.

"No, not thinkin', just knowin'," she said.

"Do you mean the pain, like I have felt, is a good thing," I asked?

"Surely, it isn't easy, but it's the depth of life that you know now, not the surface. Birth and death, they are the miracle of life, before your eyes, staring at you, giving you gifts if you can listen and be quiet."

"Is that why you like helping with babies," I asked?

"Yes, of course. It's a deeply happy time. But I'm also not afraid of helping with the dying. It is just the two ends of life, beginning and end. How you live in between is what counts."

"Hum. Births seem so much happier."

"Yes, that's sure. But both birth and death give us the chance to feel the wonder that life is."

Her smile soothed me and I felt her quiet love. Life seems to be offering me gifts and I feel ready to accept them. Every day is a gift, and as we get closer to the west, I can feel it in my bones. Time to sleep.

Love, Me

Mama Quail and her babies

Thursday, August 19, 1852

Dear Carrie,

I'm so much stronger. I have muscles in my arms and legs and back that give me a feeling of power and energy and make me feel so alive. I can feel the strength in my legs as I run and move, and when I ride Burt, as we ride and ride. My strong arms carry wood, drive the wagon, unload the wagon each night, reload it each day.

Oh the wonder of the human body. Did you ever think of it? Is there a limit to how strong we could be? Grandmama would be so upset with me, saying I'm not at all "lady-like."

Guess I'm not, from her definition. But here, in the west, we'll have to make up a new meaning for what ladies are like. Out here, it is good to be strong.

An excitement builds inside me now, a new feeling and yet it's familiar, recognizable. Am I making any sense at all? Maybe not.

Oh Carrie, if you could just see the vastness here, the fresh open wildness. I sense a wildness in me, too. A love of things pure, innocent, untouched. This must be what Papa meant when he talked about the frontier.

I looked up frontier in the dictionary. It means the edge of something. I'm on the edge of the world every day and the edge of my own frontier, of what I've known before. My body is new, my feelings are different, my thoughts open up to new vistas, too.

For all the pain and heart ache that brought me to this moment, I'm glad I'm here, right here, right now.

All love from the frontier, Katie

Friday, August 20, 1852

We left Fort Hall and are traveling now along the Snake River. We passed a towering waterfall, called American Falls. Peter, Aurelie and I stood at the edge and looked over. It was scary, but oh so exciting.

They say the Indians here are not as friendly as the Snake Indians.

We have watch at night now and people are really nervous. We are afraid that they might steal our oxen or horses. Or raid our camp and steal *us*. But so far, all is well. I pray that we pass through here peacefully. Nellie makes me feel safer in the wagon because she's an excellent watchdog.

Love, Me

Saturday, August 21, 1852

Not much time to write—I have to help a lot with baby Sharon because Aunt Sarah is so tired. But I have to write some exciting news! Peter and I found a baby antelope that had lost her mama. We're trying to talk Uncle Peter and Aunt Sarah into letting us keep her.

Peter is mad about her and she follows him around everywhere. We gave her some of Rose's milk and some grass. Nellie likes her—she licked the antelope when it was curled up to sleep. We're praying that we get to keep her. We're all so worn out and she seems to cheer us up, especially Peter. And when he is happy, then my life is easier.

Tired and dirty but another day closer to the west, as Mrs. O'Malley would say.

Love, Me

Sunday, August 22, 1852

Oh the best of the best! Uncle Peter said we can keep our baby pet. At first he said no, but then he softened. He really is a lot like Papa, gentle and kind. He saw what a difference it made with Peter.

Peter named her Little Sioux. Uncle Peter lectured us about how she might not make it, but I am thrilled to help her survive. She cries out whenever Peter is away from her.

Baby Sharon grows strong and healthy. She's already three weeks old. Such a blessing to have new life and the joy it brings.

Love, Me

Monday, August 23, 1852

We crossed the Raft River, one of the landmarks in our guidebook. After our noon break, we bade a heartfelt goodbye to the three families going on to Oregon. We took the left junction, down towards California. Aurelie's family is still with us, but I miss the folks that felt so much like family.

Peter had to say goodbye to his best friend, Luke. I think it brought back losing Mama and Papa because he cried and cried. I held him tight and then told him that I'd help him write letters to Luke, just like I write to Carrie. And that someday he'd get letters back. And maybe we could travel up to see them too, later, when we were older. That seemed to settle him down.

Then Little Sioux stood close to him and nuzzled him. He started to pet her—I think it is a her—and I knew he'd be okay. Time to sleep,
Love, Me

Little Sioux

Tuesday, August 24, 1852

Mrs. O'Malley and I gathered some wild currants at our nooning rest and then after supper and the chores, I helped her make them into jam. We put some on a biscuit to try it out. Oh so good, and still warm from the making.

I'm feeling a bit blue today. I guess that's normal. Many people are tired and feeling the strain of the journey. But we all try to stay strong for each other and don't talk about it much.

Little Sioux and Peter cheer me up though, when I see them cavorting around. They are alike–both so skinny and sturdy at the same time. He sleeps well for all the running around during the day.
Got to sleep before another long day.
Love, Me

Wednesday, August 25, 1852

Dear Carrie,

Mama taught me to write what I see and feel. There is so much that is new and amazing. Nature is my teacher now. Mama passed the job on to her and she's a beautiful schoolmistress.

Did you know that the word nature comes from the Latin root nasci, to be born? That means something to me. Living so powerfully in nature's presence, I have been born and reborn.

Every day she points out something astounding to my hungry eyes and ears. Shadows on water or rocks, sunrises bursting with orange across the landscape, sunsets lavender and soft pink against the dark hills and green trees. Mama birds with fledglings, teaching them to fly, a tree growing straight out of a rock. How can that be? If a tree can survive that, I can grow up straight too.

We're traveling along the Cassia Creek, a pure stream that gives us good water and feeds our spirits, too. The gurgling stream talks to me as we walk alongside it, encouraging me to just keep going, it will all be worth it when we're done.

But walking, walking, walking, some days I'm dreary with walking.

Hoping for a surge of energy soon, especially before the long desert ahead. Missing you from here.

All Love, Katie

Thursday, August 26, 1852

The moon lit up the dark sky this morning as we arose in the dark. I was helping Aunt Sarah with baby Sharon, who fussed a lot last night. I put her in the sling and walked her around, enjoying the fresh morning air and quiet of the day before everyone else was up and about.

The animals fed on the plentiful grass and except for their crunching and shuffling, all was quiet. Baby Sharon quieted down, too. I took her around and showed her Baby Sioux, sleeping next to our wagon and Tom, munching away down by the stream. Then we petted Burt, who seemed happy for the attention.

We saw a pair of eagles on the ridge, just as the sun began to come up. I told Sharon that was very good luck. I was supposed to be calming her down from her fitful night, but she actually helped me feel inspired again. The newness of her life fills me with energy when my own energy flags from the long days.

We passed Cathedral Rocks today. I want to sketch them, with their twin spires towering up. Mama showed me a drawing of a cathedral like that from France. My warm thoughts of Mama make my heart ache. Oh, just to be held in her arms again. I so long for that.

Love, Me

Cathedral Rocks

Friday August 27, 1852

We arrived at Goose Creek, after traveling through a broad and lovely valley.

Mr. Brown says we're headed southwest now, down to California. The terrain is very dry, almost desert-like, with sagebrush. I like the smell of the sagebrush and we use it for fires. It has kind of a sweet smell. Someone said that the Indians use it for ceremonies.

Though the streams are little here, the grass and water are plentiful for us and for the animals. I got some clean, but still feel dirty. The creek was so shallow, I couldn't get under the water but could only splash off. Oh to soak in a hot bath again. I helped Aunt Sarah wash the diapers from baby Sharon, a task we have to do every time we get near water. We hang them up to dry at night and then in the wagon during the day.

Uncle Peter brought in a jackrabbit for dinner. We found some greens and wild onions and cooked them up with the rabbit. It tasted delicious. Everything tastes as wild as the places we're in, but I'm used to that now and like it.

We have to watch out for rattlesnakes. Burt almost stepped on one when we were out riding. He reared up and we passed right over him, but it frightened me. I can still hear that dry rattle and it makes me shiver. I'm so grateful Burt didn't get hurt. I couldn't bear to lose him.

We're headed to the Humboldt River and the great desert. My lips are chapped and dry. Time to sleep.

Love, Me

Saturday, August 28, 1852

We're all baked to a crisp. There is a deep weariness to the bones. Can I ever quench my thirst for rest? And water? I notice that baby Sharon, the little antelope, Peter and Rose–the young and fresh–have energy and they give me hope and strength during these hard times.

The Indians here are called Diggers because they dig for roots. They also eat grasshoppers and other insects. Uncle Peter says to watch out for Rose and Little Sioux, so we tether them near us at night. I hear their sweet noises and am comforted. Nellie helps us to keep watch, too, as always. Sweet Nellie. Burt would whinny too, if there was danger. He's such a smart horse and he watches out for us.

Time to sleep—have to rest up for the long trek ahead in the desert. We'll have to walk all night.

Love, Me

Monday, August 30, 1852

We had a short church service yesterday, then pushed on to make time. We're following Mary's River now. The guidebook warns of the monotony of this river valley. One woman, stories say, refused to go on at this point and even set fire to the wagon in her fury. She eventually got settled down, but I can imagine the frustration and weariness that could lead to such a scene.

We have good water and grass along the river. That's a blessing, at least. We're going slow and easy to prepare for the desert up ahead. We will have to walk all through the night to cross it. We always stop before the animals get too tired out. That helps us too. Papa would like that.

Love, Me

Wednesday, September 1, 1852

Little Sioux gets fatter and spunkier every day and entertains us with her lively antics. She clearly thinks Peter is her mama now and he loves the new role. Her presence gives an air of delight and wonder to the otherwise dreary routine.

Baby Sharon is already over a month old and is chubby and cute. She smiles now and pays attention when I talk to her. She always did, I think, but now her eyes focus more. She even has a little color from the sun because we carry her in the sling.

I can't write as often with all the chores and driving the wagon, but I miss writing so, when I can't.

Love, Me

Sunday, September 5, 1852

I want to try to make the time to write, even if I am tired. And I do get so tired now, nearing the end of this long journey. But at least I can think about writing, and then when I can, I write it down.

The hillsides are gray in color with the sagebrush plant. I like the strong sharp smell of it as our wheels crush it. We're camped now in the sink of Mary's River. Grass and water plentiful and we're preparing for the long and hard pull across the desert.

Mr. Brown has us resting, mending wagons, cutting some grass and filling every possible water container. The preacher has us filling up our spirits to carry us along when we're too tired to go on, so we're singing hymns while we work.

Love, Me

The desert

Tuesday, September 7- Wednesday September 8, 1852

We began at sunrise, Tuesday, stopped to noon, ate and rested. Then began again at 3pm and went till 8pm. After we rested one hour, we walked again from 9pm till midnight.

We passed the boiling springs about 1am, Wednesday. Mr. Bret had ridden ahead and damned the flow, so the water could cool enough for the oxen to have a sip. The smell of sulfur turned my stomach.

141

We rested a bit, then walked all night, slow and steady. About 4am, we came to a sandy span in which the oxen sank down to their knees. I cried to watch them pulling and straining, so tired already. Many oxen before us died here and we had to pass by their bodies and bones. I kept talking to ours, telling them they were almost there.

Folks were letting go of any unnecessary items, even ones which were cherished, more china and trunks. Thank you, Papa, for making us travel light. We already let go of our things back home, so we didn't have to leave them alongside the trail.

We passed a trading post selling water for 75 cents a bucket. We bought five, but mostly to give to the animals. Peter and I kept encouraging them, feeding them on the cut grass from the wagons.

We pushed on. We had to get through the desert before the heat of the day. Our cow, Rose, nearly gave out and Peter and I had to coax her on with little gulps of water from a bucket we held out in front of her. We reached the ridge, just as the sun came up, and could see the cottonwoods along the river, down the sagebrush-covered slope.

At that point, the animals smelled the water, so we unhitched them and let them run on down. They ran right into the river and stood, bawling, drinking and soaking. Little Sioux came through easily. She just followed Peter all the way. He gave her bits of grass and as much water as we could spare.

We didn't lose even one animal and I think it is because we've taken it slow and easy all along, as Papa wanted us to. I will never forget the sight of so many dead oxen from other wagon trains and my stomach turns at the thought of it now.

I am thankful. The worst is over now and we will rest here for a few days, preparing for the Sierra Nevada Mountains.

The river is pure and cold and we drink and drink, savoring the pleasure of the clear, cool water.

It's hard to think we have another difficult hurdle—the mountains, but it will be our last.

Love, Me

Thursday, September 9, 1852

I had a bath—cold and clear water, but it felt good to let it soak into my skin, just like our animals did after the desert. My skin feels so dry and hardened–like leather. But there is joy in knowing we are closer now to the end of our long journey, and everyone is hopeful.

Sierra Nevada means "snowy mountains." We're praying that we get through them before the snow. They look like gray granite walls touching the clouds and I have no idea how we'll ever get over them. Others have gone before us though. We all pray for clear skies and strength.

Tired and clean,

Love, Me

The Sierra Nevada Mountains

Friday, September 10, 1852

A rescue party of men came out to help us over the pass. They brought us flour, bacon, coffee and much news. But most of all, they renewed our hope, that we're close to the end of our journey.

They all looked so fresh, clean and their horses so lively and quick. What a weary group we are. My clothes look about how I feel, torn and tattered, faded and worn.

A young man named Jack, who is eighteen, has been especially good to Peter. Jack lost his little brother to cholera last year when he came west. He's fun to talk to, a new friend. Soon we will all say good-bye. I don't want to lose this dear family.

Even Noah's Pa has softened and has asked forgiveness for his anger and temper. The preacher is happy and so is Noah.

Mrs. O'Malley has been helping me to take in one of mama's dresses so that when we have a celebration at the end, I'll have something pretty to wear. When we first took it out of the trunk, it smelled so much like Mama that I cried. Mrs. O'Malley let me cry on her shoulder.

"They should be here with us—to know that we're going to make it," I said.

"Yes, love, they should be," she said, handing me her hanky. "And you know what?" She lifted up my chin and looked into my eyes. "They are."

I want to think of them here with us. I have to think of that or it feels lonely again. Snuggling into my warm quilt and tired. Love, Me

Friday, September 10, 1852
Dear Carrie,

It is clearly fall now. Winter's chill creeps into the nights and predawn. I still stay cozy in my quilt and featherbed, grandma's wool cap, gloves and mittens. Will we have a warm

home before winter sets in? I sorely hope so. And yet, at times, I feel as though I could live forever now, out in the wild, with but a canvas cover over my head.

I helped Mrs. O'Malley pick blackberries and wild currants for her pies. Such a treat. We ate it warm with some of Rose's fresh cream. I seem to appreciate the simple things even more now after all these months of walking–the taste of the tart berries and the rich cream. The smiles of all of those who enjoyed the pie and their gratitude that we made them.

People are anxious to get to the end of the journey. With the end clearly in sight, I'm savoring the last bits of this amazing chapter of my life. I so miss Mama and Papa, now that we're near the end. I miss you, too, and can't wait to soon read one of your letters.

All love, Katie

Saturday, September 11, 1852

I helped Mrs. O'Malley make loads of pies. I used Mama's medicine bottle to roll some dough out into crusts. I'm so much slower than Mrs. O'Malley, but I'm learning. I had a chance to talk to her some.

"I don't want it to end, this time together, the adventure, the wildness, the excitement."

"Yes, I know. But each ending means a new beginning, too, you know," she said, smiling at me with her clear blue eyes.

"But I'm used to the journey now, our life as I know it. I'm not sure I want to live in a house again. And I can't imagine a house without Mama and Papa."

"Well, I can understand all that. But I have an idea. The parts that you love the most, those are qualities to keep in your life, in your new beginning. Bring the joy of the journey in your heart wherever you are. You know, sometimes I miss my home

145

in Ireland. But when I do, I bring the happiness I knew there to where I am, and it's ever so good."

"Oh Mrs. O'Malley, you always have the right words to say to me."

"And you the ears to hear them. Now aren't you quite the baker with those crusts you've just rolled out. Let's get some berries into them and set them to cooking."

She always calms my heart. In joy,
Love, Me

Monday, September 13, 1852

We said goodbye to our Indian guide and the river and are heading through Dog Valley, up and down mountainsides. I'm thankful we rested up along the Truckee River to prepare for this.

People's spirits soar at being so close now. The nights are cool under the down coverlet and we're cozy in the wagon. There's growing excitement that the end of our journey is within our grasp. The difficulties of the steep mountains are balanced by the amazement that we are almost there, we've almost done it.

There's a spirit now of peacefulness as we climb our last and most difficult mountain. Yet this is where many have failed. We see their remnants, left behind. Wagons, furniture, the skeletons of dead oxen, graves hastily made and left behind.

We sing most nights now. Even for a few minutes, around the fire. It's a way to be quiet and also to give thanks for our own successful journey so far.

Climbing the hills, Mr. Bret plays his harmonica and the song passes along the train, the ones in the front giving life to the ones in the back as the song carries through the air and wafts on the breezes, through the steep rock walls and echoes down the canyons. Peter joins in with his harmonica—he knows lots of songs now and so loves to play. Baby Sioux follows him along happily.

It will take us many days to cross these mountains.

Love, Me

Tuesday, September 14, 1852

We wind along through huge pine forests, grassy meadows and see many deer. We're taking it slow and easy. It helps so to have some new supplies, full bellies, lots of water and also to be clean.

We just have the mountain pass to go now. Clear skies with the highest point of the pass just ahead. I can't see how we can get over it. The guidebook suggests strategies and it helps to know that others have gone ahead of us. The men in the rescue party have done it before and offer such help. Burt is frisky in the fresh mountain air and from being with the fresh horses of our guides. Excited!

Love, Me

Wednesday, September 15, 1852

It took three days to get up to the top of the pass, much pulling with ropes and doubling up the teams. Everyone walked to spare the animals. I put Nellie into the wagon—she is so light. She is tired and her feet are sore and she enjoys the ride. Then in the evening, she can run around a bit.

I carried Baby Sharon, who is so plump and jolly now. She is six weeks old already. I told her that she was walking over the mountains of California and that someday people would read about this in books and she would be famous because she was there. She looked at me, gurgled and then promptly fell asleep. I hope the books I write don't put people to sleep, but then I would like to write lullaby stories, too.

Just before we started down, Aurelie, Peter, Jack and I ran up to the highest spot to see the view. As we looked back to the east, we could see the dry and desolate desert. Then ahead, forest covered hills rolling down toward the west. We all stood close together in the awe of what it meant—we were in California now. Could that really be possible? We raced back down the hill, yelling and shrieking.

Going downhill, the men tied the ropes around trees to help lower the wagons and stop the downhill pull. The poor trees got big burns into their trunks, which will be a testimony of our passing for many years to come. We're going to rest and say goodbye in a few days.

The days are warm, the nights cold. Last night the water froze in the bucket. No sign of any storms. The clear sky is such a blessing. People are crying in relief and joy. Slow going pulling the wagons up and over. Everyone working together well, though. Can we almost be there?

Love, Me

Thursday, Sept 16, 1852
Dear Carrie,

We're resting along the shore of a large and beautiful lake. The lake sits so quiet, except for the birds and a few ducks on the early morning water. So much clean, cool water, after so much dry, desolate desert. The lakes here are crystal clear, blue green, all the way to the bottom. Not brown like at home. Midday, I jump in with Peter and Aurelie and my new friend Jack. When I open my eyes under water, I can see!

The days are warm, but the nights get to be freezing.

We're staying one day to celebrate being over the summit. It's only a few days downhill from here. Can you believe that we are almost there?

We're going to split up soon. Some go northwest to the gold camps area, others go southwest to Sacramento City. But today we celebrated. Our rescue party supplied us with eggs, flour, butter, fruits–peaches, plums, and grapes. We're feasting.

Peter caught some fresh fish from the lake and we're making fresh peach and blackberry pies. Peter and I picked the wild mountain blackberries from the vines near the lake. Rose, bless her, gave us her daily milk and cream, even after 2,000 miles, so we had fresh cream again for on top.

The men who came to greet us were mighty grateful to us. They hadn't had a fresh pie in months. We were grateful to them and so glad to talk to some new folks full of news of California and our future life. We just kept feeding them and they just kept talking. It was a good exchange. We're as hungry for news as they are for fresh fixings.

Mrs. O'Malley did her part for sure. She turned out 12 pies in just over three hours–using other's ovens. She says she's practicing for her future business–fixing food for the miners. She'll be a rousing success, I bet.

They say a fresh pie will go for $1 and a fresh meal the same. She's got the real gold claim if you ask me, because she's sure of hers. The others aren't–it's all fancy and hopes, though some have really struck it rich.

There aren't many women out here it seems. Not only do men pay top dollar for home-cooked food, they line up for hours just to catch a glimpse of a woman. That makes me feel embarrassed!

Oh Carrie, can we really almost be there? I long to share these moments with you and am glad at least to do it on paper.

*Love and hugs from the Sierra Nevada mountains—my first
letter to you from California!*
Love, Katie

One of my pies with fresh cream from Rose on top

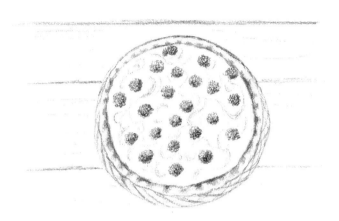

Friday, September 17, 1852

I awakened this morning to the cries of geese as they head
south for the winter. Such a haunting sound, reminding me of
the power of nature and the changing of the seasons. How do the
geese know that it is time to go? So many questions that I wish I
could ask Mama or Papa.

The sunlight dances its reflection on the granite rocks. The
squirrels leave footprints in the sand and one peeks out at me
from behind an almond shaped rock. How tiny and agile he is
as he sprints across the clearing. His friend joins him and for a
moment they play, then set back to work preparing for winter.

The camp rests quiet in the dawn light. As I sit here and face
the day, I look back on our journey across the mountains. So
many mountains, so many miles of desert and plains. So much
we've seen and felt and so many tears have stained my dusty
cheeks.

But today I'm clean, no longer dusty. Mama and Papa–it's not such a painful sore anymore, but there is a scar in my heart. Right now, I can feel them here and I miss them.

We'd be laughing and playing in this clear mountain lake. Mama would be smiling, breathing in the fresh air and might say, "Katie, this is what we came for. You can feel the open spaces here. There have been very few humans here in this place. We must respect it and leave as little trace of our passing as we can." I will remember that Mama.

Papa would have been quiet, but his spirit would have brimmed over with joy as he looked around at the towering pines touching the bright clear sky. I can feel his emotion at the depth here, the possibility and the friendliness of the natural plenty all around us.

I am soothed and cared for here. Thank you, God for bringing us to this place. I don't know why you took Mama and Papa and I pray that I will understand your reasons someday. And I pray that if I don't understand, I will not lose faith.

This moment, I feel as quiet and yet as alive and moving as this lake. Let me never find an end to the depth of this joy or to the fullness of love to express in my life.

Love, Me

The geese on their way south

Sunday, Sept. 19, 1852
Dear Carrie,

It's not just my body which has grown on this journey. I am bigger inside, too. That's a part of a person which no one can measure. The quiet inside and out soothes me. This old pine near me has seen and felt a lot. I have now, too.

I've experienced towering mountains, roaring rivers, still lakes, icy black nights full of stars. I feel as if each place we passed, I carry inside of me. Each one has given me back a piece of myself along the way. It's been like a treasure hunt, into the future, discovering parts I never knew I'd lost.

As a duck glides through the water, the ripples angle out like two giant feathers in a V shape behind. The trees and rocks appear reflected in the water, shimmering, ghostly images of themselves, thrust up from the underworld, haunting them of what they could become. Now the lake is gray-green.

I've got to run and help out with the morning chores. I feel so much more grown up, like my roots go deeper into the ground. I've grown deep and not just up. Mrs. Oak would be proud. Give her a big hug from me. Love from your cousin, Katie

Monday, September 20, 1852

I have fun with Jack. He's a real good listener. I've talked to him about losing Mama and Papa. He listens like there's no one else in the whole world. I like that. He lost his aunt and little brother to the cholera, so his family hurts too. It's made those of us who are left more alive. We've looked death in the eyes. Life is more vivid to me now.

I love to dance with him, too. We twirl and fly around, then stop breathless, laughing. He's my best friend right now, along with Aurelie. It's nice to have a new friend, but I'll never forget all that Aurelie and I have shared these past five months. Still, it is special to talk to Jack. He also likes to read, like me, so we can talk about the books we love.

I'm going to miss him when he goes. His family goes to Sacramento City and we go toward the gold camps. We're going to try to write, but he's not even sure where he'll be. He's taller than I am, which is tall, has brown eyes and dark brown hair.

I watched the dawn this morning, rich with pinks and lavenders, then quickly flat-grays, yellows, then just blue sky. A duck family nestles along the banks near me.

Mother Nature has shown me one lesson over and over, gently, quietly. You have to catch the gifts in life when they're offered. They're fleeting, then gone. I may not understand why a gift is being offered now. If I'm not paying attention, it's too late.

I feel the precious gift of this moment, from life to me. Alone with my soul, these ducks, this lake and the early morning light, I accept this gift and the light and peace that fill my soul. Love, Me

The little duck family

Later morning:
Monday, September 20, 1852
Dear Carrie,

I'm adding onto my letter from Sunday and will mail it when we arrive in the gold camps. Then you will be able to write me back there. I am so excited to receive your letters. There is even a chance one has arrived already.

We're still at the lake—we leave today. The water shimmers bright now, silvery yellow, gold and silver all at once. The cloudbank hides the sun, which glows out from behind. Here comes the duck family.

The mama duck glides proudly, then a little distance behind her follow her six baby ducks. She guards them, keeping them in her sight always. She murmurs soft throaty calls to them as they continue their morning pilgrimage around the lake, feeding, floating, blending into the morning light and ripples of the lake.

The sun shines brightly on the lake now. Two large beams emanating from a billowy cream puff cloud, behind the purple, blue mountain.

I awoke refreshed this morning. I felt like myself again, the first time in months that I hadn't felt as if I was awakening from a bad dream. I have calmed and quieted my soul.

I have stilled and quieted my soul...Psalms 131:2

Now the sun sits much higher, rising above the clouds to reach the blue sky. It must be how Noah feels to be getting out from under the cloud of his Pa's anger.

Papa told me that a person can survive difficult times if they're strong inside. That those times can make them discover how strong they really are. No matter how hard it seems, life can be offering you gifts all the time, but you have to look for the gifts.

That seems to be the challenge. It's like all the men who are rushing out to California to search for gold. They sift through a lot of sand to find one nugget.

Papa said life is like that too. But the nuggets are there for those bright of eye and strong of heart and purpose. Yes, Papa, now I see.

Time to push on today. Late start, another baby born. Precious moments of stillness, broken by the shrill cry of new life calling out to us, a little boy. They'll call him Donner, named after the mountain pass we just went over and the family that perished there six years ago. So much to be grateful for.

Much love from my heart to yours,

Your cousin, Katie

Tuesday, September 21, 1852

Another beautiful morning as the sun rises in the east. I feel a cool breeze on my face as we continue to descend the mountains. A river gleams ahead, a silver-blue ribbon shining in the light. Grassy meadows and trees. I could live in a valley like this—it feels like home.

Over the top and down, we're heading to the end of our journey. Mrs. O'Malley and her family will be going with us to the gold mine area. I'm so glad. I couldn't bear to say good-bye to her.

Everyone agreed to celebrate our success last night—our last night together. We camped by another clear lake. The water is cold and the shimmering leaves of the cottonwoods and aspens look like gold coins and fall as I watch, reminding me of winter creeping in, day by day.

There was much joy, celebration, jubilation, and tears. Mrs. O'Malley put on her best cotton dress and took off her apron for the dancing. She made ginger cakes for everyone with the last bit of things, but that doesn't matter now. We're only a few days from supplies of all we need.

I love the crisp clear air here. The tall trees seem to touch the very stars at night.

I wore Mama's dress that we had taken in. It felt so special to feel pretty and clean. I danced with Peter, Jack, Aurelie, Mr. Brown and Mrs. O'Malley. Such fun. I snuck away from the dancing for a few moments and just sat. The harvest moon was huge and yellow and lit up the still lake, reflecting the trees. I felt very quiet inside, peaceful, joyful and full, as vast as the sky in that moment.

The dance of life. We spin and turn, laugh and smile and then stop. I hugged my knees to my chest and noticed how my body had changed. My legs are longer, my chest is fuller, my arms are longer, too. Even my hair falls down longer as it warms my back in the cool night air.

I'm growing up and I like how I feel, how it feels, the world and me. What lies ahead: A new home, a new life, a new state. I feel ready.

I will always remember how it looked last night—the sky, the stars, the moon on the lake. That moment is frozen in time, a picture that I will carry in my heart and cherish always.

Almost to my new home,

Love, Me

Wednesday, September 22, 1852

Papa was right to have us come here. I can feel the freedom, as if I can breathe it in the deep gulps of fine fresh air that tingle my lungs. How did he know that it would be like this?

Yes, Papa, you were right. This place feels like it was worth the journey and all that we went through to get here.

Today we said goodbye to Jack and the others who helped us over the pass. Just one man stayed with us to show us the trail. Tonight, we will camp at a ranch on the way and then tomorrow arrive in the gold camps. Aurelie and her family come with us. And of course, Mrs. O'Malley. I can't imagine my life without her now.

Peter runs along excited and Little Sioux trots along beside him. I can ride Burt now freely because there is no more danger of Indians and everyone is used to me riding now, too. Tom pulls, faithful as always, and Rose follows. Nellie runs or rides—I keep an eye on her to notice if she is tiring out.

I carry baby Sharon most of the time when I'm walking. She is a comfort to me when she snuggles up to me, her head on my heart. She looks around with wide eyes at the trees and the sky.

Mama and Papa would be proud at how we all made it through. Our wagon is mostly empty now—we've used up all the provisions and just have Mama's trunk with our few clothes and books. And of course, the seeds and acorns we brought along.

Where will we end up and how will we pass the winter? I don't know. I guess I'm more comfortable with the unknown than I ever was. It's as if I can hear the wind swaying the tall pines and whispering to me as we're passing through. *It will be alright. A good life is ahead. You're strong and able. Do not be afraid.*

I'm not afraid, I whisper back to the wind and the trees. *Thank you for your help.*

I'm going to walk with Mrs. O'Malley the last few miles to our new home.

The End

Acknowledgements

Special thanks go out to:

Carol Nimick and her 6th grade class at the Waldorf Charter school, for allowing me to read Katie's story to them.

Readers Maria Brower, Heather Williams, granddaughters Maggie and Lilah Hayes, grandchildren Hunter and Ireland Williams, Cheryl Murray and Emily Murray Mackenzie.

David A. Comstock for his helpful advice.
All the helpful staff at the Doris Foley Historical Library in Nevada City, where I spent countless hours reading diaries and asking questions. If there are any historical errors, they are mine.

Children's librarian Rachel Tucker for her valuable encouragement.

Margie Baxley for the layout and Margaret Campbell for the cover layout.

And always, my husband Landon Carter, who supports and encourages me to get my writing out into the world.

And to you, dear readers. Thank you for reading this story. I am so grateful.

About the author

Diane Covington-Carter is an award-winning and best-selling author who has written three memoirs. This is her first work of fiction.

She lives in Northern California on an organic apple farm and off the grid in New Zealand.

Visit her website at: www.dianecovingtoncarter.com

37091595R00089

Made in the USA
San Bernardino, CA
27 May 2019